POEMS.

BY THE AUTHOR OF "A LIFE FOR A LIFE," "JOHN HALIFAX, GENTLEMAN," &c.

BOSTON:
TICKNOR AND FIELDS.
MDCCCLX.

AUTHOR'S EDITION.

RIVERSIDE, CAMBRIDGE:
STEREOTYPED AND PRINTED BY
H. O. HOUGHTON AND COMPANY.

TO

HENRY BLACKETT, Esq.

A TOKEN OF RESPECT AND ESTEEM

FROM AUTHOR TO PUBLISHER.

PREFACE.

Many of these Poems, extending over a period of ten years, have appeared anonymously in "Chambers' Journal" and elsewhere. The frequent reprinting of them, here and in America, has induced the author to collect, select, revise, and claim — her errant children.

Whether they were worth collecting, and are really "*Poems*," public opinion must decide.

CONTENTS.

SONNETS.

POEMS.

PHILIP MY KING.

"Who bears upon his baby brow the round
And top of sovereignty."

LOOK at me with thy large brown eyes,
Philip my king,
Round whom the enshadowing purple lies
Of babyhood's royal dignities:
Lay on my neck thy tiny hand
With love's invisible sceptre laden;
I am thine Esther to command
Till thou shalt find a queen-handmaiden,
Philip my king.

O the day when thou goest a wooing,
Philip my king!
When those beautiful lips 'gin suing,
And some gentle heart's bars undoing
Thou dost enter, love-crown'd, and there
Sittest love-glorified. Rule kindly,

Tenderly, over thy kingdom fair,
For we that love, ah! we love so blindly,
    Philip my king.

Up from thy sweet mouth — up to thy brow,
    Philip my king!
The spirit that there lies sleeping now
May rise like a giant and make men bow
As to one heaven-chosen amongst his peers:
My Saul, than thy brethren taller and fairer
Let me behold thee in future years; —
Yet thy head needeth a circlet rarer,
    Philip my king.

— A wreath not of gold, but palm. One day,
    Philip my king,
Thou too must tread, as we trod, a way
Thorny and cruel and cold and gray:
Rebels within thee and foes without,
Will snatch at thy crown. But march on, glorious,
Martyr, yet monarch: till angels shout
As thou sit'st at the feet of God victorious,
    "Philip the king!"

THOUGHTS IN A WHEAT-FIELD.

"The harvest is the end of the world, and the reapers are the angels."

In his wide fields walks the Master,
In his fair fields, ripe for harvest,
Where the evening sun shines slant-wise
On the rich ears heavy bending;
    Saith the Master: "It is time."
Though no leaf shows brown decadence,
And September's nightly frost-bite
Only reddens the horizon,
"It is full time," saith the Master,
    The wise Master, "It is time."

Lo, he looks. That look compelling
Brings his labourers to the harvest;
Quick they gather, as in autumn
Passage-birds in cloudy eddies
    Drop upon the sea-side fields;
White wings have they, and white raiment,
White feet shod with swift obedience,
Each lays down his golden palm-branch,

And uprears his sickle shining,
    "Speak, O Master — is it time?"

O'er the field the servants hasten,
Where the full-stored ears droop downwards,
Humble with their weight of harvest:
Where the empty ears wave upward,
    And the gay tares flaunt in rows:
But the sickles, the sharp sickles,
Flash new dawn at their appearing,
Songs are heard in earth and heaven,
For the reapers are the angels,
    And it is the harvest time.

O Great Master, are thy footsteps
Even now upon the mountains?
Art thou walking in thy wheat-field?
Are the snowy-wingèd reapers
    Gathering in the silent air?
Are thy signs abroad, the glowing
Of the distant sky, blood-redden'd —
And the near fields trodden, blighted,
Choked by gaudy tares triumphant, —
    Sure, it must be harvest time?

Who shall know the Master's coming?
Whether it be at dawn or sunset,

When night dews weigh down the wheat-ears,
Or while noon rides high in heaven,
    Sleeping lies the yellow field?
Only, may thy voice, Good Master,
Peal above the reapers' chorus,
And dull sound of sheaves slow falling, —
" Gather all into My garner,
    For it is My harvest time."

IMMUTABLE.

"With whom is no variableness, neither shadow of turning."

Autumn to winter — winter into spring —
Spring into summer — summer into fall —
So rolls the changing year, and so we change;
Motion so swift, we know not that we move.
Till at the gate of some memorial hour
We pause — look in its sepulchre to find
The cast-off shape that years since we called "I" —
And start, amazed. Yet on! we may not stay
To weep or laugh. All which is past, is past:
Even while we gaze the simulated form
Drops into dust, like many-centuried corpse
At opening of a tomb.

Alack, this world
Is full of change, change, change — nothing but change!
Is there not one straw in life's whirling flood
To hold by, as the torrent sweeps us down,
Us, scattered leaves; eddied and broken; torn
Roughly asunder; or in smooth mid-stream

Divided each from other without pain;
Collected in what looks like union,
Yet is but stagnant chance — stopping to rot
By the same pebble till the tide shall turn;
Then on, to find no shelter and no rest,
For ever rootless and for ever lone.
O God, we are but leaves upon Thy stream,
Clouds on Thy sky. We do but move across
The silent breast of Thine infinitude
Which bears us all. We pour out day by day
Our long, brief moan of mutability
To Thine immutable — and cease.

Yet still
Our change yearns after Thine unchangedness:
Our mortal craves Thine immortality;
Our manifold and multiform and weak
Imperfectness, requires the perfect ONE.
For Thou art ONE, and we are all of Thee;
Dropped from Thy bosom, as Thy sky drops down
Its morning dews, which glitter for a space,
Uncertain whence they fell, or whither tend,
Till the great Sun arising on his fields
Upcalls them all, and they rejoicing go.

So, with like joy, O Light Eterne, we spring
Thee-ward, and leave the pleasant fields of earth,

Forgetting equally its blossom'd green
And its dry dusty paths which drank us up
Remorseless — we, poor humble drops of dew,
That only wish'd to freshen a flower's breast,
And be exhaled to heaven.

O Thou supreme
All-satisfying and immutable One,
It is enough to be absorbed in Thee
And vanish — though 't were only to a voice
That through all ages with perpetual joy
Goes evermore loud crying, "God! God! God!"

FOUR YEARS.

At the midsummer, when the hay was down,
Said I, mournfully — My life is at its prime,
Yet bare lie my meadows, shorn before the time,
In my scorch'd woodlands the leaves are turning
brown.
It is the hot midsummer, and the hay is down.

At the midsummer, when the hay was down,
Stood she by the streamlet, young and very fair,
With the first white bindweed twisted in her hair —
Hair that drooped like birch-boughs, — all in her
simple gown.
For it was midsummer, — and the hay was down.

At the midsummer, when the hay was down,
Crept she, a willing bride, close into my breast:
Low piled the thunder clouds had drifted to the
west —

Red-eyed out glared the sun, like knight from lea-
guered town,
That eve in high midsummer, when the hay was
down.

It is midsummer — all the hay is down;
Close to her bosom press I dying eyes,
Praying, "God shield thee till we meet in Para-
dise!"
Bless her in Love's name who was my brief life's
crown, —
And I go at midsummer, when the hay is down.

THE DEAD CZAR.

Lay him beneath his snows,
The great Norse giant who in these last days
Troubled the nations. Gather decently
The imperial robes about him. 'T is but man —
This demi-god. Or rather it *was* man,
And is — a little dust, that will corrupt
As fast as any nameless dust which sleeps
'Neath Alma's grass or Balaklava's vines.

No vineyard grave for him. No quiet tomb
By river margin, where across the seas
Children's fond thoughts and women's memories come
Like angels, to sit by the sepulchre,
Saying: "All these were men who knew to count,
Front-faced, the cost of honour, nor did shrink
From its full payment: coming here to die,
They died — like men."

But this man? Ah! for him
Funereal state, and ceremonial grand,

The stone-engraved sarcophagus, and then
Oblivion.

Nay, oblivion were as bliss
To that fierce howl which rolls from land to land
Exulting — "Art thou fallen, Lucifer,
Son of the morning?" or condemning — "Thus
Perish the wicked!" or blaspheming — "Here
Lies our Belshazzar, our Sennacherib,
Our Pharaoh — he whose heart God hardenèd,
So that he would not let the people go."

Self-glorifying sinners! Why, this man
Was but like other men: — you, Levite small,
Who shut your saintly ears, and prate of hell
And heretics, because outside church-doors,
Your church-doors, congregations poor and small
Praise Heaven in their own way; — You, autocrat
Of all the hamlets, who add field to field
And house to house, whose slavish children cower
Before your tyrant footstep; — you, foul-tongued
Fanatic or ambitious egotist,
Who thinks God stoops from His high majesty
To lay His finger on your puny head,
And crown it — that you henceforth may parade
Your maggotship throughout the wondering world —
"I am the Lord's anointed!"

Fools and blind!
This Czar, this emperor, this disthronèd corpse,
Lying so straightly in an icy calm
Grander than sovereignty, was but as ye —
No better and no worse; — Heaven mend us all!

Carry him forth and bury him. Death's peace
Rest on his memory! Mercy by his bier
Sits silent, or says only these few words, —
"Let him who is without sin 'mongst ye all
Cast the first stone."

THE WIND AT NIGHT.

O SUDDEN blast, that through this silence black
    Sweeps past my windows,
Coming and going with invisible track
    As death or sin does —

Why scare me, lying sick, and, save thine own,
    Hearing no voices?
Why mingle with a helpless human moan
    Thy mad rejoices?

Why not come gently, as good angels come
    To souls departing,
Floating among the shadows of the room
    With eyes light-darting,

Bringing faint airs of balm that seem to rouse
    Thoughts of a Far Land,
Then binding softly upon weary brows
    Death's poppy-garland?

O fearful blast, I shudder at thy sound,
Like heathen mortal
Who saw the Three that mark life's doomèd bound
Sit at his portal.

Thou might'st be laden with sad, shrieking souls,
Carried unwilling
From their known earth to the unknown stream
that rolls
All anguish stilling.

Fierce wind, will the Death-angel come like thee,
Soon, soon to bear me
—*Whither?* what mysteries may unfold to me,
What terrors scare me?

Shall I go wand'ring on through empty space
As on earth, lonely?
Or seek through myriad spirit-ranks one face,
And miss that only?

Shall I not then drop down from sphere to sphere
Palsied and aimless?
Or will my being change so, that both fear
And grief die nameless?

Rather I pray Him who Himself is Love,
Out of whose essence

We all do spring, and towards Him tending, move
Back to His presence,

That even His brightness may not quite efface
The soul's earth-features,
That the dear human likeness each may trace
Glorified creatures;

That we may not cease loving, only taught
Holier desiring;
More faith, more patience; with more wisdom fraught,
Higher aspiring.

That we may do all work we left undone
Here — though unmeetness;
From height to height celestial passing on
Towards full completeness.

Then, strong Azrael, be thy supreme call
Soft as spring-breezes,
Or like this blast, whose loud fiend-festival
My heart's blood freezes,

I will not fear thee. If thou safely keep
My soul, God's giving,
And my soul's soul, I, wakening from death-sleep,
Shall first know living.

A FABLE.

SILENT and sunny was the way
    Where Youth and I danced on together:
So winding and embowered o'er,
We could not see one rood before.
Nevertheless all merrily
We bounded onward, Youth and I,
    Leashed closely in a silken tether:
      (Well-a-day, well-a-day!)
Ah Youth, ah Youth, but I would fain
See thy sweet foolish face again!

It came to pass, one morn of May,
    All in a swoon of golden weather,
That I through green leaves fluttering
Saw Joy uprise on Psyche wing:
Eagerly, too eagerly
We followed after — Youth and I —
    Till suddenly he slipped the tether:
      (Well-a-day, well-a-day!)

"Where art thou, Youth?" I cried. In vain;
He never more came back again.

Yet onward through the devious way
In rain or shine, I recked not whether,
Like many another maddened boy
I tracked my Psyche-wingèd Joy;
Till, curving round the bowery lane,
Lo — in the pathway stood pale Pain,
And we met face to face together:
(Well-a-day, well-a-day!)
"Whence comest thou?" — and I writhed in vain —
"Unloose thy cruel grasp, O Pain!"

But he would not. Since, day by day
He has ta'en up Youth's silken tether
And changed it into iron bands.
So through rich vales and barren lands
Solemnly, all solemnly
March we united, he and I;
And we have grown such friends together
(Well-a-day, well-a-day!)
I and this my brother Pain,
I think we'll never part again.

LABOUR IS PRAYER.

LABORARE est orare:
  We, black-visaged sons of toil,
From the coal-mine and the anvil
  And the delving of the soil, —
From the loom, the wharf, the warehouse,
  And the ever whirling mill,
Out of grim and hungry silence
  Raise a weak voice small and shrill; —
Laborare est orare:
  Man, dost hear us? God, He will.

We who just can keep from starving
  Sickly wives — not always mild:
Trying not to curse Heaven's bounty
  When it sends another child, —
We who, worn-out, doze on Sundays
  O'er the Book we strive to read,
Cannot understand the parson
  Or the catechism and creed.

Laborare est orare: —
  Then, good sooth, we pray indeed.

We, poor women, feeble-natured,
  Large of heart, in wisdom small,
Who the world's incessant battle
  Cannot understand at all,
All the mysteries of the churches,
  All the troubles of the state, —
Whom child-smiles teach "God is loving,"
  And child-coffins, "God is great:"
Laborare est orare: —
  We too at His footstool wait.

Laborare est orare;
  Hear it, ye of spirit poor,
Who sit crouching at the threshold
  While your brethren force the door;
Ye whose ignorance stands wringing
  Rough hands, seam'd with toil, nor dares
Lift so much as eyes to heaven —
  Lo! all life this truth declares,
Laborare est orare;
  And the whole earth rings with prayers.

A SILLY SONG.

"O HEART, my heart!" she said, and heard
His mate the blackbird calling,
While through the sheen of the garden green
May rain was softly falling—
Aye softly, softly falling.

The butter-cups across the field
Made sunshine rifts of splendour:
The round snow-bud of the thorn in the wood
Peep'd through its leafage tender,
As the rain came softly falling.

"O heart, my heart!" she said and smiled,
"There 's not a tree of the valley,
Or a leaf I wis which the rain's soft kiss
Freshens in yonder alley,
Where the drops keep ever falling,—

"There 's not a foolish flower i' the grass,
Or bird through the woodland calling,
So glad again of the coming of rain
As I of these tears now falling —
These happy tears down falling."

IN MEMORIAM.

Obiit 1854.

Heaven rest thee!
We shall go about to-day
In our festal garlands gay;
Whatsoever robes we wear
Not a trace of black be there.
Well, what matters? none is seen
On thy daisy covering green,
Or thy pure white pillow, hid
Underneath a coffin lid.
Heaven rest thee!

Heaven take thee!—
Aye, heaven only. Sleeps beneath
One who died a virgin death:
Died so slowly, day by day,
That it scarcely seemed decay,
Till this lonely churchyard kind
Opened—and we left behind

Nothing but a little dust;—
Heaven is pitiful and just:
Heaven take thee!

Heaven keep thee:
Nevermore above the ground
Be one relic of thee found:
Lay the turf so smooth, we crave,
None would guess it was a grave,
Save for grass that greener grows,
Or for wind that gentlier blows
All the earth o'er, from this spot
Where thou wert—and thou art not.
Heaven keep thee!

AN HONEST VALENTINE.

Returned from the Dead-letter Office.

THANK ye for your kindness,
  Lady fair and wise,
Though love 's famed for blindness,
  Lovers — hem ! for lies.
Courtship 's mighty pretty,
  Wedlock a sweet sight ; —
Should I (from the city,
  A plain man, Miss —) write,
Ere we spouse-and-wive it,
  Just one honest line,
Could you e'er forgive it,
  Pretty Valentine ?

Honey-moon quite over,
  If I less should scan
You with eye of lover
  Than of mortal man ?
Seeing my fair charmer
  Curl hair spire on spire,

All in paper armour,
  By the parlour fire;
Gown that wants a stitch in
  Hid by apron fine,
Scolding in her kitchen, —
  O fie, Valentine!

Should I come home surly
  Vex'd with fortune's frown,
Find a hurly burly,
  House turn'd upside down,
Servants all a-snarl, or
  Cleaning steps or stair:
Breakfast still in parlour,
  Dinner — anywhere:
Shall I to cold bacon
  Meekly fall and dine?
No — or I 'm mistaken
  Much, my Valentine.

What if we should quarrel?
  — Bless you, all folks do: —
Will you take the war ill
  Yet half like it too?
When I storm and jangle,
  Obstinate, absurd,
Will you sit and wrangle

Just for the last word, —
Or, while poor Love crying
Upon tip-toe stands,
Ready plumed for flying —
Will you smile, shake hands,
And the truth beholding,
With a kiss divine
Stop my rough mouth's scolding ? —
Bless you, Valentine !

If, should times grow harder,
We have lack of pelf,
Little in the larder,
Less upon the shelf;
Will you, never tearful,
Make your old gowns do,
Mend my stockings, cheerful,
And pay visits few ?
Crave nor gift nor donor,
Old days ne'er regret,
Seek no friend save Honour,
Dread no foe but Debt ;
Meet ill-fortune steady,
Hand to hand with mine,
Like a gallant lady —
Will you, Valentine ?

Then, whatever weather
  Come — or shine, or shade,
We 'll set out together,
  Not a whit afraid.
Age is ne'er alarming —
  I shall find, I ween,
You at sixty charming
  As at sweet sixteen:
Let 's pray, nothing loath, dear,
  That our funeral may
Make one date serve both, dear,
  As our marriage day.
Then, come joy or sorrow,
  Thou art mine — I thine.
So we 'll wed to-morrow,
  Dearest Valentine.

LOOKING DEATH IN THE FACE.

Ay, in thy face, old fellow! Now 's the time.
The Black Sea wind flaps my tent-roof, nor wakes
These lads of mine, who take of sleep their fill,
As if they thought they 'd never sleep again,
Instead of —
Pitiless Crimean blast,
How many a howling lullaby thou 'lt raise
To-morrow night, all nights till the world's end,
Over some sleepers here!
Some? — *who?* Dumb Fate
Whispers in no man's ear his coming doom;
Each thinks — "not I — not I."
But thou, grim Death,
I hear thee on the night-wind flying abroad,
I feel thee here, squatted at our tent-door,
Invisible and incommunicable,
Pointing:
"Hurrah!"
Why yell so in your sleep,

Comrade? Did *you* see aught?
Well — let him dream:
Who knows, to-morrow such a shout as this
He 'll die with. A brave lad, and very like
His sister. * * * *
So! just two hours have I lain
Freezing. That pale white star, which came and peered
Through the tent-opening, has passed on, to smile
Elsewhere, or lost herself i' the dark — God knows.
Two hours nearer to dawn. The very hour —
The very hour and day, a year ago,
When we light-hearted and light-footed fools
Went jingling idle swords in waltz and reel,
And smiling in fair faces. How they 'd start
Those dainty red and white soft faces kind,
If they could but behold my visage now,
Or his — or his — or some poor faces cold
We cover'd up with earth last noon.
— There sits
The laidly Thing I felt on our tent-door
Two hours back. It has sat and never stirred
I cannot challenge it — or shoot it down,
Or grapple with it, as with that young Russ
Whom I killed yesterday. (What eyes he had! —
Great limpid eyes, and curling dark-red hair —
A woman's picture hidden in his breast —

I never liked this fighting hand to hand.)
No — it will not be met like flesh and blood,
This shapeless, voiceless, immaterial Thing,
Yet I *will* meet it. Here I sit alone —
Show me thy face, O Death!
There, there. I think
I did not tremble.
I am a young man;
Have done full many an ill deed, left undone
Many a good one: lived unto the flesh,
Not to the spirit: I would rather live
A few years more, and try if things might change.
Yet, yet I hope I do not tremble, Death;
And that thy finger pointed at my heart
But calms the tumult there.

What small account
The All-living seems to take of this thin flame
Which we call *life*. He sends a moment's blast
Out of war's nostrils, and a myriad
Of these our puny tapers are blown out
For ever. Yet we shrink not — we, such frail
Poor knaves, whom a spent ball can instant strike
Into eternity — we helpless fools,
Whom a serf's clumsy hand and clumsier sword
Smiting — shall sudden into nothingness

Let out that something rare which could conceive
A universe and its God.

Free, open-eyed,
We rush like bridegrooms to Death's grisly arms:
Surely the very longing for that clasp
Proves us immortal. Immortality
Alone could teach this mortal how to die.
Perhaps, war is but Heaven's great ploughshare, driven
Over the barren, fallow earthly fields,
Preparing them for harvest; rooting up
Grass, weeds, and flowers, which necessary fall,
That in these furrows the wise Husbandman
May drop celestial seed.
So let us die;
Yield up our little lives, as the flowers do;
Believing He 'll not lose one single soul —
One germ of His immortal. Nought of His
Or Him can perish; therefore let us die.

I half remember, something like to this
She says in her dear letters. So — let 's die.
What, dawn? The faint hum in the trenches fails —
Is that a bell i' the mist? My faith, they go
Early to matins in Sebastopol! —

A gun! — Lads — stand to your arms; the Russ is
here.

Agnes.

Kind heaven, I have look'd Death in the face,
Help me to die.

BY THE ALMA RIVER.

WILLIE, fold your little hands;
    Let it drop, that "soldier" toy:
Look where father's picture stands —
    Father, who here kiss'd his boy
Not two months since — father kind,
Who this night may — Never mind
Mother's sob, my Willie dear,
Call aloud that He may hear
Who is God of battles, say,
"Oh, keep father safe this day
    By the Alma river."

Ask no more, child. Never heed
    Either Russ, or Frank, or Turk,
Right of nations or of creed,
    Chance-poised victory's bloody work:
Any flag i' the wind may roll
On thy heights, Sebastopol;
Willie, all to you and me
Is that spot, where'er it be,

Where he stands — no other word!
Stands — God sure the child's prayer heard —
By the Alma river.

Willie, listen to the bells
Ringing through the town to-day.
That 's for victory. Ah, no knells
For the many swept away —
Hundreds — thousands! Let us weep,
We who need not — just to keep
Reason steady in my brain
Till the morning comes again,
Till the third dread morning tell
Who they were that fought and *fell*
By the Alma river.

Come, we 'll lay us down, my child,
Poor the bed is, poor and hard;
Yet thy father, far exiled,
Sleeps upon the open sward,
Dreaming of us two at home:
Or beneath the starry dome
Digs out trenches in the dark,
Where he buries — Willie, mark —
Where *he buries* those who died
Fighting bravely at his side
By the Alma river.

Willie, Willie, go to sleep,
    God will keep us, O my boy;
He will make the dull hours creep
    Faster, and send news of joy,
When I need not shrink to meet
Those dread placards in the street,
Which for weeks will ghastly stare
In some eyes — Child, say thy prayer
Once again; a different one:
Say, "O God, Thy will be done
    By the Alma river."

ROTHESAY BAY.

Fu' yellow lie the corn-rigs
Far doun the braid hill-side;
It is the brawest harst field
Alang the shores o' Clyde, —
And I'm a puir harst-lassie
That stan's the lee-lang day
Shearing the corn-rigs of Ardbeg
Aboon sweet Rothesay Bay.

O I had ance a true-love —
Now, I hae nane ava;
And I had ance three brithers,
But I hae tint them a'
My father and my mither
Sleep i' the mools this day.
I sit my lane amang the rigs
Aboon sweet Rothesay Bay.

It 's a bonnie bay at morning,
And bonnier at the noon,

But it 's bonniest when the sun draps
    And red comes up the moon:
When the mist creeps o'er the Cumbrays,
    And Arran peaks are grey,
And the great black hills, like sleepin' kings,
    Sit grand roun' Rothesay Bay,

Then a bit sigh stirs my bosom,
    And a wee tear blin's my e'e —
And I think o' that far Countrie
    What I wad like to be!
But I rise content i' the morning
    To wark while wark I may
I' the yellow harst field of Ardbeg
    Aboon sweet Rothesay Bay.

LIVING:

AFTER A DEATH.

"That friend of mine who lives in God."

O LIVE!
(Thus seems it we should say to our beloved —
Each held by such slight links, so oft removed;)
And I can let thee go to the world's end,
All precious names, companion, love, spouse, friend,
Seal up in an eternal silence grey,
Like a closed grave till resurrection-day:
All sweet remembrances, hopes, dreams, desires,
Heap, as one heaps up sacrificial fires:
Then, turning, consecrate by loss, and proud
Of penury — go back into the loud
Tumultuous world again with never a moan —
Save that which whispers still, "My own, my own,"
Unto the same broad sky whose arch immense
Enfolds us both like the arm of Providence:
And thus, contented, I could live or die,
With never clasp of hand or meeting eye

On this side Paradise.—While thee I see
Living to God, thou art alive to me.

O live!
And I, methinks, can let all dear rights go,
Fond duties melt away like April snow,
And sweet, sweet hopes, that took a life to weave,
Vanish like gossamers of autumn eve.
Nay, sometimes seems it I could even bear
To lay down humbly this love-crown I wear,
Steal from my palace, helpless, hopeless, poor,
And see another queen it at the door—
If only that the king had done no wrong,
If this my palace, where I dwelt so long,
Were not defiled by falsehood entering in:—
There is no loss but change, no death but sin,
No parting, save the slow corrupting pain
Of murder'd faith that never lives again.

O live!
(So endeth faint the low pathetic cry
Of love, whom death has taught love cannot die,)
And I can stand above the daisy bed,
The only pillow for thy dearest head,
There cover up for ever from my sight
My own, my earthly all of earth delight;
And enter the sea-cave of widow'd years,

Where far, far off the trembling gleam appears
Through which thy heavenly image slipped away,
And waits to meet me at the open day.
Only to me, my love, only to me.
This cavern underneath the moaning sea;
This long, long life that I alone must tread,
To whom the living seem most like the dead,—
Thou wilt be safe out on the happy shore:
He who in God lives, liveth evermore.

IN OUR BOAT.

Stars trembling o'er us and sunset before us,
Mountains in shadow and forests asleep;
Down the dim river we float on for ever,
Speak not, ah breathe not — there 's peace on the deep.
Come not, pale Sorrow, flee till to-morrow,
Rest softly falling o'er eyelids that weep;
While down the river we float on for ever,
Speak not, ah breathe not, there 's peace on the deep.
As the waves cover the depths we glide over,
So let the past in forgetfulness sleep,
While down the river we float on for ever,
Speak not, ah breathe not, there 's peace on the deep.
Heaven shine above us, bless all that love us,
All whom we love in thy tenderness keep!
While down the river we float on for ever,
Speak not, ah breathe not, there 's peace on the deep.

THE RIVER SHORE.

For an old tune of Dowland's.

WALKING by the quiet river
  Where the slow tide seaward goes,
All the cares of life fall from us,
  All our troubles find repose:
Nought forgetting, nought regretting,
  Lovely ghosts from days no more
Glide with white feet o'er the river,
  Smiling towards the silent shore.

So we pray in His good pleasure
  When this world we 've safely trod,
We may walk beside the river
  Flowing from the throne of God:
All forgiving, all believing,
  Not one lost we loved before,
Looking towards the hills of heaven
  Calmly from the eternal shore.

A FLOWER OF A DAY.

OLD friend, that with a pale and pensile grace
Climbest the lush hedgerows, art thou back again,
Marking the slow round of the wond'rous years?
Didst beckon me a moment, silent flower?

Silent? As silent is the archangel's pen
That day by day writes our life chronicle,
And turns the page; the half-forgotten page,
Which all eternity will never blot.

Forgotten? No, we never do forget:
We let the years go: wash them clean with tears,
Leave them to bleach, out in the open day,
Or lock them careful by, like dead friends' clothes,
Till we shall dare unfold them without pain —
But we forget not, never can forget.

Flower, thou and I a moment face to face —
My face as clear as thine, this July noon

Shining on both, on bee and butterfly
And golden beetle creeping in the sun —
Will pause, and lifting up, page after page,
The many-colour'd history of life,
Look backwards, backwards.

So, the volume close!
This July day, with the sun high in heaven,
And the whole earth rejoicing — let it close.

I think we need not sigh, complain, nor rave;
Nor blush — our doings and misdoing all
Being more 'gainst heaven than man, heaven them does keep
With all its doings and undoings strange
Concerning us. — Ah, let the volume close:
I would not alter in it one poor line.

My dainty flower, my innocent white flower
With such a pure smile looking up to heaven,
With such a bright smile looking down on me —
(Nothing but smiles — as if in all the world
Were no such things as thunderstorms or frosts,
Or broken petals trampled on the ground,
Or shivering leaves whirled in the wintry air
Like ghosts of last year's joys:) — my pretty flower,
I'll pluck thee — smiling too. Not one salt drop

Shall stain thee: — if these foolish eyes are dim,
'T is only with a wondering thankfulness
That they behold such beauty and such peace,
Such wisdom and such sweetness, in God's world.

THE NIGHT BEFORE THE MOWING.

All shimmering in the morning shine
  And diamonded with dew,
And quivering in the scented wind
  That thrills its green heart through, —
The little field, the smiling field,
  With all its flowers a-blowing,
How happy looks the golden field
  The day before the mowing!

All still 'neath the departing light,
  Twilight, though void of stars,
Save where, low westering, Venus hides
  From the red eye of Mars;
How quiet lies the silent field
  With all its beauties glowing;
Just stirring — like a child asleep, —
  The night before the mowing.

Sharp steel, inevitable hand,
  Cut keen, cut kind! Our field

We know full well must be laid low
  Before its wealth it yield:
Labour and mirth and plenty blest
  Its blameless death bestowing:
And yet we weep, and yet we weep,
  The night before the mowing.

PASSION PAST.

Were I a boy, with a boy's heart-beat
At glimpse of her passing adown the street,
Of a room where she had enter'd and gone,
Or a page her hand had written on—
Would all be with me as it was before?
Oh no, never! no, no, never!
Never any more.

Were I a man, with a man's pulse-throb,
Breath hard and fierce, held down like a sob,
Dumb, yet hearing *her* lightest word,
Blind, until only *her* garment stirr'd:
Would I pour my life like wine on her floor?
No, no, never: never, never!
Never any more.

Grey and wither'd, wrinkled and marr'd,
I have gone through the fire and come out unscarr'd,
With the image of manhood upon me yet,

No shame to remember, no wish to forget:
But could she rekindle the pangs I bore?—
Oh no, never: thank God, never!
Never any more.

Old and wrinkled, wither'd and grey—
And yet if her light step pass'd to-day,
I should see her face all faces among,
And say—"Heaven love thee, whom I loved long!
Thou hast lost the key of my heart's door,
Lost it ever, and for ever,
Ay, for evermore."

OCTOBER.

IT is no joy to me to sit
  On dreamy summer eves,
When silently the timid moon
  Kisses the sleeping leaves,
And all things through the fair hush'd earth
  Love, rest — but nothing grieves.
Better I like old autumn
  With his hair toss'd to and fro,
Firm striding o'er the stubble fields
  When the equinoctials blow.

When shrinkingly the sun creeps up
  Through misty mornings cold,
And Robin on the orchard hedge
  Sings cheerily and bold,
While heavily the frosted plum
  Drops downwards on the mould; —
And as he passes, autumn
  Into earth's lap does throw

Brown apples gay in a game of play,
  As the equinoctials blow.

When the spent year its carol sinks
  Into a humble psalm,
Asks no more for the pleasure draught,
  But for the cup of balm,
And all its storms and sunshine bursts
  Controls to one brave calm, —
Then step by step walks autumn,
  With steady eyes that show
Nor grief nor fear, to the death of the year,
  While the equinoctials blow.

MOON-STRUCK.

A FANTASY.

It is a moor
Barren and treeless; lying high and bare
Beneath the archèd sky. The rushing winds
Fly over it, each with his strong bow bent
And quiver full of whistling arrows keen.

I am a woman, lonely, old, and poor.
If there be any one who watches me
(But there is none) adown the long blank wold,
My figure painted on the level sky
Would startle him as if it were a ghost, —
And like a ghost, a weary wandering ghost,
I roam and roam, and shiver through the dark
That will not hide me. O for but one hour,
One blessed hour of warm and dewy night,
To wrap me like a pall — with not an eye
In earth or heaven to pierce the black serene.

Night, call ye this? No night; no dark — no rest —
A moon-ray sweeps down sudden from the sky,
And smites the moor —
Is 't thou, accursèd Thing,
Broad, pallid, like a great woe looming out —
Out of its long-seal'd grave, to fill all earth
With its dead ghastly smile? Art there again,
Round, perfect, large, as when we buried thee,
I and the kindly clouds that heard my prayers?
I 'll sit me down and meet thee face to face,
Mine enemy! — Why didst thou rise upon
My world — my innocent world, to make me mad?
Wherefore shine forth, a tiny tremulous curve
Hung out in the grey sunset beauteously,
To tempt mine eyes — then nightly to increase
Slow orbing, till thy full, blank, pitiless stare
Hunts me across the world?
No rest — no dark.
Hour after hour that passionless bright face
Climbs up the desolate blue. I will press down
The lids on my tired eye-balls — crouch in dust,
And pray.
— Thank God, thank God! — a cloud has hid
My torturer. The night at last is free:
Forth peep in crowds the merry twinkling stars.
Ah, we 'll shine out, the little silly stars
And I; we 'll dance together across the moor,

They up aloft — I here. At last, at last
We are avengèd of our adversary!

The freshening of the night air feels like dawn.
Who said that I was mad? I will arise,
Throw off my burthen, march across the wold
Airily — Ha, what, stumbling? Nay, no fear —
I am used unto the dark, for many a year
Steering companionless athwart the waste
To where, deep hid in valleys of white mist,
The pleasant home-lights shine. I will but pause,
Turn round and gaze —
O me! O miserable me!
The cloud-bank overflows: sudden out-pour
The bright white moon-rays — ah, I drown, I drown,
And o'er the flood, with steady motion, slow
It walketh — my inexorable Doom.

No more: I shall not struggle any more:
I will lie down as quiet as a child, —
I can but die.
There, I have hid my face:
Stray travellers passing o'er the silent wold
Would only say "She sleeps."
Glare on, my Doom;
I will not look at thee: and if at times

I shiver, still I neither weep nor moan:
Angels may see, I neither weep nor moan.

Was that sharp whistling wind the morning breeze
That calls the stars back to the obscure of heaven?
I am very cold. — And yet there is a change.
Less fiercely the sharp moonbeams smite my brain,
My heart beats slower, duller: soothing rest
Like a soft garment binds my shuddering limbs. —
If I looked up now, should I see it still
Gibbeted ghastly in the hopeless sky? —
No!
            It is very strange: all things seem strange:
Pale spectral face, I do not fear thee now:
Was 't this mere shadow which did haunt me once
Like an avenging fiend? — Well, we fade out
Together: I 'll nor dread nor curse thee more.

How calm the earth seems! and I know the moor
Glistens with dew-stars. I will try and turn
My poor face eastward. Close not, eyes! That light
Fringing the far hills, all so fair — so fair,
Is it not dawn? I am dying, but 't is dawn.
"*Upon the mountains I behold the feet*
Of my Beloved: let us forth to meet" —
Death.

This is death. I see the light no more;
I sleep.
But like a morning bird my soul
Springs singing upward, into the deeps of heaven
Through world on world to follow Infinite Day.

A STREAM'S SINGING.

O HOW beautiful is Morning!
How the sunbeams strike the daisies,
And the king-cups fill the meadow
Like a golden-shielded army
    Marching to the uplands fair;—
I am going forth to battle,
And life's uplands rise before me,
And my golden shield is ready,
And I pause a moment, timing
My heart's pæan to the waters,
As with cheerful song incessant
    Onwards runs the little stream;
Singing ever, onward ever,
    Boldly runs the merry stream.

O how glorious is Noon-day!
With the cool large shadows lying
Underneath the giant forest,
The far hill-tops towering dimly
    O'er the conquered plains below;—

I am conquering — I shall conquer
In life's battle-field impetuous:
And I lie and listen dreamy
To a double-voiced, low music, —
Tender beech-trees sheeny shiver
Mingled with the diapason
    Of the strong, deep, joyful stream,
Like a man's love and a woman's;
    So it runs — the happy stream!

O how grandly cometh Even,
Sitting on the mountain summit,
Purple-vestured, grave, and silent,
Watching o'er the dewy valleys,
    Like a good king near his end: —
I have laboured, I have govern'd;
Now I feel the gathering shadows
Of the night that closes all things:
And the fair earth fades before me,
And the stars leap out in heaven,
While into the infinite darkness
    Solemn runs the stedfast stream —
Onward, onward, ceaseless, fearless,
    Singing runs the eternal stream.

A REJECTED LOVER.

You "never loved me," Ada. These slow words,
Dropp'd softly from your gentle woman-tongue
Out of your true and kindly woman-heart,
Fell, piercing into mine like very swords
The sharper for their kindness. Yet no wrong
Lies to your charge, nor cruelty, nor art,
Ev'n while you spoke, I saw the tender tear-drop
start.

You "never loved me." No, you never knew,
You, with youth's morning fresh upon your soul,
What 't is *to love:* slow, drop by drop, to pour
Our life's whole essence, perfumed through and
through
With all the best we have or can control
For the libation — cast it down before
Your feet — then lift the goblet, dry for evermore.

I shall not die as foolish lovers do:
A man's heart beats beneath this breast of mine,

The breast where — Curse on that fiend-whispering
"*It might have been!*" — Ada, I will be true
Unto myself — the self that so loved thine:
May all life's pain, like these few tears that spring
For me, glance off as rain-drops from my white
dove's wing!

May you live long, some good man's bosom-flower,
And gather children round your matron knees:
So, when all this is past, and you and I
Remember each our youth-days as an hour
Of joy — or anguish, one, serene, at ease,
May come to meet the other's stedfast eye,
Thinking, "He loved me well!" clasp hands, and so
pass by.

A LIVING PICTURE.

No, I 'll not say your name. I have said it now,
As you mine, first in childish treble, then
Up through a score and more familiar years
Till baby-voices mock us. Time may come
When your tall sons look down on our white hair,
Amused to hear us call each other thus,
And question us about the old, old days,
The far-off days, the days when we were young.

How distant do they seem, and yet how near!
Now, as I lie and watch you come and go,
With garden basket in your hand; in gown
Just girdled, and brown curls that girl-like fall,
And straw hat flapping in the April breeze,
I could forget this lapse of years — start up
Laughing — "Come, let 's go play!"
Well-a-day, friend,
Our play-days are all done.
Still, let us smile:
For as you flit about your garden here

You look like this spring morning: on your lips
An unseen bird sings snatches of gay tunes,
While, an embodied music, moves your step,
Your free, wild, springy step, like Atala's,
Or Pocahontas, careless child o' the sun —
Those Indian beauties I compare you to —
I, still your praiser, —
Nay, nay, I 'll not praise,
Fair seemeth fairest, ignorant 't is fair:
That light incredulous laugh is worth a world!
That laugh, with childish echoes.
So then, fade,
Mere dream. Come, true and sweet reality:
Come, dawn of happy wifehood, motherhood,
Ripening to perfect noon! Come, peaceful round
Of simple joys, fond duties, gladsome cares,
When each full hour drops bliss with liberal hand
Yet leaves to-morrow richer than to-day.

Will you sit here? the grass is summer-warm.
Look at those children making daisy-chains,
So did we too, do you mind? That eldest lad
He has your very mouth. Yet, you will have 't
His eyes are like his father's? Perhaps so:
They could not be more dark and deep and kind.
Do you know, this hour I have been fancying you
A poet's dream, and almost sigh'd to think

There was no poet to praise you —
Why, you 're flown
After those mad elves in the flower-beds there,
Ha — ha — you 're no dream now.
Well, well — so best!
My eyelids droop content o'er moistened eyes:
I would not have you other than you are.

LEONORA.

LEONORA, Leonora,
How the word rolls — *Leonora* —
Lion-like, in full-mouth'd sound,
Marching o'er the metric ground
With a tawny tread sublime —
So your name moves, Leonora,
Down my desert rhyme.

So you pace, young Leonora,
Through the alleys of the wood,
Head erect, majestic, tall,
The fit daughter of the Hall:
Yet with hazel eyes declined,
And a voice like summer wind,
And a meek mouth, sweet and good,
Dimpling ever, Leonora,
In fair womanhood.

How those smiles dance, Leonora.
As you meet the pleasant breeze
Under your ancestral trees:
For your heart is free and pure
As this blue March sky o'erhead,
And in the life-path you tread,
All the leaves are budding, sure,
All the primroses are springing,
All the birds begin their singing —
'T is your spring-time, Leonora,
May it long endure.

But it *will* pass, Leonora:
And the silent days must fall
When a change comes over all:
When the last leaf downward flitters,
And the last, last sunbeam glitters
On the terraced hill-side cool,
On the peacocks by the pool:
When you 'll walk along these alleys
With no lightsome foot that dallies
With the violets and the moss, —
But with quiet steps and slow,
And grave eyes that earthward grow,
And a matron-heart inured
To all women have endured, —

Must endure and ever will,
All the joy and all the ill,
All the gain and all the loss —
Can you cheerfully lay down
Careless girlhood's flowery crown,
And thus take up, Leonora,
Womanhood's meek cross?

Ay! your eyes shine, Leonora,
Warm, and true, and brave. and kind:
And although I nothing know
Of the maiden heart below,
I in them good omens find.
Go, enjoy your present hours
Like the birds and bees and flowers:
And may summer days bestow
On you just so much of rain,
Blessed baptism of pain!
As will make your blossoms grow.
May you walk, as through life's road
Every noble woman can, —
With a pure heart before God,
And a true heart unto man:
Till with this same smile you wait
For the opening of the Gate
That shuts earth from mortal eyes;

Till at last, with peaceful heart,
All contented to depart,
Leaving children's children playing
In these woods you used to stray in,
You may enter, Leonora,
Into Paradise.

PLIGHTED.

Mine to the core of the heart, my beauty!
Mine, all mine, and for love, not duty:
Love given willingly, full and free,
Love for love's sake — as mine to thee.
Duty 's a slave that keeps the keys,
But Love, the master, goes in and out
Of his goodly chambers with song and shout,
Just as he please — just as he please.

Mine, from the dear head's crown, brown-golden,
To the silken foot that 's scarce beholden;
Give to a few friends hand or smile,
Like a generous lady, now and awhile,
But the sanctuary heart, that none dare win,
Keep holiest of holiest evermore;
The crowd in the aisles may watch the door,
The high-priest only enters in.

Mine, my own, without doubts or terrors,
With all thy goodnesses, all thy errors,

Unto me and to me alone reveal'd,
"A spring shut up, a fountain seal'd."
  Many may praise thee — praise mine as thine,
Many may love thee — I 'll love them too;
But thy heart of hearts, pure, faithful, and true,
  Must be mine, mine wholly, and only mine.

Mine! — God, I thank Thee that Thou hast given
Something all mine on this side heaven:
Something as much myself to be
As this my soul which I lift to Thee:
  Flesh of my flesh, bone of my bone,
Life of my life, whom Thou dost make
Two to the world for the world's work's sake —
  But each unto each, as in Thy sight, *one.*

MORTALITY.

"And we shall be changed."

Ye dainty mosses, lichens grey,
  Press'd each to each in tender fold,
And peacefully thus, day by day,
  Returning to their mould;

Brown leaves, that with aërial grace
  Slip from your branch like birds a-wing,
Each leaving in the appointed place
  Its bud of future spring; —

If we, God's conscious creatures, knew
  But half your faith in our decay,
We should not tremble as we do
  When summon'd clay to clay.

But with an equal patience sweet
  We should put off this mortal gear,

In whatsoe'er new form is meet
  Content to re-appear.

Knowing each germ of life He gives
  Must have in Him its source and rise,
Being that of His being lives
  May change, but never dies.

Ye dead leaves, dropping soft and slow,
  Ye mosses green and lichens fair,
Go to your graves, as I will go,
  For God is also there.

LIFE RETURNING.

After War-time.

O LIFE, dear life, with sunbeam finger touching
  This poor damp brow, or flying freshly by
  On wings of mountain wind, or tenderly
In links of visionary embraces clutching
  Me from the yawning grave —
Can I believe thou yet hast power to save?

I see thee, O my life, like phantom giant
  Stand on the hill-top, large against the dawn,
  Upon the night-black clouds a picture drawn
Of aspect wonderful, with hope defiant,
  And so majestic grown
I scarce discern the image as my own.

Those mists furl off, and through the vale resplendent
  I see the pathway of my years prolong:

Not without labour, yet for labour strong:
Not without pain, but pain whose touch transcendent
By love's divinest laws
Heart unto heart, and all hearts upwards, draws.

O life, O love, your diverse tones bewildering
Make silence, like two meeting waves of sound;
I dream of wifely white arms, lisp of children —
Never of ended wars,
Save kisses sealing honourable scars.

No more of battles! save the combat glorious
To which all earth and heaven may witness stand;
The sword of the Spirit taking in my hand
I shall go forth, since in new fields victorious
The King yet grants that I
His servant live, or His good soldier die.

MY FRIEND.

My Friend wears a cheerful smile of his own,
  And a musical tongue has he;
We sit and look in each other's face,
  And are very good company.
A heart he has, full warm and red
  As ever a heart I see;
And as long as I keep true to him,
  Why, he 'll keep true to me.

When the wind blows high and the snow falls fast
  And we hear the wassailers' roar —
My Friend and I, with a right good-will
  We bolt the chamber door:
I smile at him and he smiles at me
  In a dreamy calm profound,
Till his heart leaps up in the midst of him
  With a comfortable sound.

His warm breath kisses my thin grey hair
  And reddens my ashen cheeks;

He knows me better than you all know,
  Though never a word he speaks: —
Knows me as well as some had known
  Were things — not as things be.
But hey, what matters? my Friend and I
  Are capital company.

At dead of night, when the house is still,
  He opens his pictures fair:
Faces that are, that used to be,
  And faces that never were:
My wife sits sewing beside my hearth,
  My little ones frolic wild,
Though — Lillian 's married these twenty years,
  And I never had a child.

But hey, what matters? when those who laugh
  May weep to-morrow, and they
Who weep be as those that wept not — all
  Their tears long wiped away.
I shall burn out, like you, my Friend,
  With a bright warm heart and bold,
That flickers up to the last — then drops
  Into quiet ashes cold.

And when you flicker on me, old Friend,
  In the old man's elbow-chair,

Or — something easier still, where we
  Lie down, to arise up fair
And young, and happy — why then, my Friend,
  Should other friends ask of me,
Tell them I lived and loved and died
  In the best of all company.

A VALENTINE.

Ye are twa laddies unco gleg,
  An' blithe an' bonnie:
As licht o' heel as Anster's Meg; —
Gin ye 'd a lassie's favour beg,
I' faith she couldna stir a peg
  Ance lookin' on ye!

He 's a douce wiselike callant — Jim:
  Of wit aye ready.
Cuts aff ane's sentence, t' ither's limb,
An' whiles he 's daft and whiles he 's grim,
But brains? — wha 's got the like o' him
  In 's wee bit heidie?

Dear laddie wi' the curlin' hair,
  Gentlest of ony:
That gies kind looks an' speeches fair
To dour auld wives as lassies rare, —
I ken a score o' lads an' mair,
  But nane like Johnnie!

And gin ye learn the way to woo,
  Hae sweethearts mony,
O laddie, never say ye loe
An' gie fause coin for siller true;
A lassie's sair heart 's naething new, —
  Mind o' that, Johnnie.

An' dinna change your luve sae fast
  For ilk face bonnie,
Lest waefu' want track wilfu' waste,
And a' your youthfu' years lang past,
Ye get the crookit stick at last,
  Ochone, puir Johnnie!

But callants baith, tak tent, and when
  Bright e'en hae won ye,
Tak each your jo — and keep her — then
Be faithfu' as ye 're fond, ye ken,
Or — gang your gate like honest men,
  Young Jim and Johnnie.

Sae when auld Time his crookit claw
  Sall lay upon ye,
When, Jim, your feet that dance sae braw
Are no the lightest in the ha',
An' a' your curly haffets fa',
  My winsome Johnnie, —

May each his ain warm ingle view,
  Cosie as ony:
A gudewife sonsie, leal and true,
O' bonnie dochters not a few,
An' lads — sic lads as ye 're the noo —
  Dear Jim and Johnnie!

GRACE OF CLYDESIDE.

Ah, little Grace of the golden locks,
  The hills rise fair on the shores of Clyde.
As the merry waves wear out these rocks
She wears my heart out, glides past and mocks:
  But heaven's gate ever stands open wide.

The boat goes softly along, along,
  Like a river of life glows the amber Clyde;
Her voice floats near me like angels' song, —
Ah, sweet love-death, but thy pangs are strong!
  Though heaven's gate ever stands open wide.

We walk by the shore and the stars shine bright,
  But coldly, above the solemn Clyde:
Her arm touches mine — her laugh rings light —
One hears my silence: His merciful night
  Hides me — *Can* heaven be open wide?

I ever was but a dreamer, Grace:
  As the grey hills watch o'er the sunny Clyde,

Standing afar, each in his place,
I watch your young life's beautiful race,
  Apart — until heaven be opened wide.

And sometimes when in the twilight balm
  The hills grow purple along the Clyde,
The waves flow softly and very calm,
I hear all nature sing this one psalm,
  That "heaven's gate ever stands open wide."

So, happy Grace, with your spirit free,
  Laugh on! life is sweet on the banks of Clyde
This is no blame unto thee or me;
Only God saw it could not be,
  Therefore His heaven stands open wide.

TO A BEAUTIFUL WOMAN.

"A daughter of the gods: divinely tall,
And most divinely fair."

SURELY, dame Nature made you in some dream
Of old-world women — Chriemhild, or bright
Aslauga, or Boadicea fierce and fair,
Or Berengaria as she rose, her lips
Yet ruddy from the poison that anoints
Her memory still, the queen of queenly wives.

I marvel, who will crown you wife, you grand
And goodly creature! who will mount supreme
The empty chariot of your maiden heart,
Curb the strong will that leaps and foams and chafes
Still masterless, and guide you safely home
Unto the golden gate, where quiet sits
Grave Matronhood, with gracious, loving eyes.

What eyes you have, you wild gazelle o' the plain,
You fierce hind of the forest! now they flash,

Now glow, now in their own dark down-dropt shade
Conceal themselves a moment, as some thought
Too brief to be a feeling, flits across
The April cloudland of your careless soul —
There — that light laugh — and 't is full sun — full
day.

Would I could paint you, line by line, ere Time
Touches the gorgeous picture! your ripe mouth,
Your white arch'd throat, your stature like to Saul's
Among his brethren, yet so fitly framed
In such harmonious symmetry, we say
As of a cedar among common trees
Never "How tall!" but only "O how fair!"

Who made you fair? moulded you in the shape
That poets dream of; sent you forth to men
HIS caligraph inscribed on every curve
Of your brave form?
Is it written on your soul?
— I know not.
Woman, upon whom is laid
Heaven's own sign-manual, Beauty, mock heaven
not!
Reverence thy loveliness — the outward type
Of things we understand not, nor behold
But as in a glass, darkly; wear it thou

With awful gladness, grave humility,
That not contemns, nor boasts, nor is ashamed,
But lifts its face up prayerfully to heaven, —
"Thou who hast made me, make me worthy Thee!"

MARY'S WEDDING.

February 25th, 1851.

You are to be married, Mary,
  This hour as I wakeful lie
In the dreamy dawn of the morning,
  Your wedding hour draws nigh;
Miles off, you are rising, dressing,
  Your bridemaidens gay among,
In the same old rooms we played in, —
  You and I, when we were young.

Your bridemaids — they were our playmates:
  Those known rooms, every wall,
Could speak of our childish frolics,
  Loves, jealousies, great and small:
Do you mind how pansies changed we
  And smiled at the word "forget?" —
'T was a girl's romance: yet somehow
  I have kept my pansy yet.

Do you mind our poems written
  Together? our dreams of fame —
And of love — how we 'd share all secrets
  When that sweet mystery came?
It is no mystery now, Mary;
  It was unveiled, year by year,
Till — this is your marriage morning;
  And I rest quiet here.

I cannot call up your face, Mary,
  The face of the bride to-day:
You have outgrown my knowledge,
  The years have so slipp'd away.
I see but your girlish likeness,
  Brown eyes and brown falling hair; —
God knows, I did love you dearly,
  And was proud that you were fair.

Many speak my name, Mary,
  While yours in home's silence lies:
The future I read in toil's guerdon,
  You will read in your children's eyes:
The past — the same past with either —
  Is to you a delightsome scene,
But I cannot trace it clearly
  For the graves that rise between.

I am glad you are happy, Mary!
  These tears, could you see them fall,
Would show, though you have forgotten,
  I have remembered all.
And though my cup may be empty
  While yours is all running o'er,
Heaven keep you its sweetness, Mary,
  Brimming for evermore.

BETWEEN TWO WORLDS.

Parting for Australia.

Here sitting by the fire
I aspire, love, I aspire —
Not to that "other world" of your fond dreams,
But one as nigh and nigher,
Compared to which your real, unreal seems.

Together as to-night
In our light, love, in our light
Of reunited joy appears no shade:
From this our hope's reach'd height
All things are possible and level made.

Therefore we sit and view —
I and you, love, I and you —
That wondrous valley o'er southern seas,
Where in a country new
You will make for me a sweet nest of ease;

Where I, your poor tired bird,
(Nothing stirred ? Love, nothing stirred ?)
May fold her wings and be no more distrest :
Where troubles may be heard
Like outside winds at night which deepen rest.

Where in green pastures wide
We 'll abide, love, we 'll abide,
And keep content our patriarchal flocks,
Till at our aged side
Leap our young brown-faced shepherds of the rocks.

Ah, tale that 's easy told !
(Hold my hand, love, tighter hold.)
What if this face of mine, which *you* think fair —
If it should ne'er grow old,
Nor matron cap cover this maiden hair ?

What if this silver ring
(Loose it clings, love, yet does cling :)
Should ne'er be changed for any other ? nay,
This very hand I fling
About your neck should — Hush ! to-day 's to-day :

To-morrow is — ah, whose ?
You 'll not lose, love, you 'll not lose

This hand I pledged, if never a wife's hand
    For tender household use
Led by yours fearless into a far, far land.

    Kiss me and do not grieve ;
    I believe, love, I believe
That He who holds the measure of our days,
    And did thus strangely weave
Our opposite lives together, to His praise —

    He never will divide
    Us so wide, love, us so wide:
But will, whate'er befalls us, clearly show
    That those in Him allied
In life or death are nearer than they know.

COUSIN ROBERT.

O cousin Robert, far away
  Among the lands of gold,
How many years since we two met? —
  You would not like it told.

O cousin Robert, buried deep
  Amid your bags of gold —
I thought I saw you yesternight
  Just as you were of old.

You own whole leagues — I half a rood
  Behind my cottage door;
You have your lacs of gold rupees,
  And I my children four;

Your tall barques dot the dangerous seas,
  My "ship 's come home" — to rest
Safe anchor'd from the storms of life
  Upon one faithful breast.

And it would cause no start or sigh,
  Nor thought of doubt or blame,
If I should teach our little son
  His cousin Robert's name.—

That name, however wide it rings,
  I oft think, when alone,
I rather would have seen it graved
  Upon a churchyard stone—

Upon the white sunshining stone
  Where cousin Alick lies:
Ah, sometimes, woe to him that lives!
  Happy is he that dies!

O Robert, Robert, many a tear—
  Though not the tears of old—
Drops, thinking of your face last night
  Your hand's remember'd fold;

A young man's face, so like, so like
  Our mothers' faces fair:
A young man's hand, so firm to clasp,
  So resolute to dare.

I thought you good—I wish'd you great;
  You were my hope, my pride:

To know you good, to make you great
  I once had happy died.

To tear the plague-spot from your heart,
  Place honour on your brow,
See old age come in crownèd peace —
  I almost would die now!

Would give — all that 's now mine to give —
  To have you sitting there,
The cousin Robert of my youth —
  Though beggar'd, with grey hair.

O Robert, Robert, some that live
  Are dead, long ere they are old;
Better the pure heart of our youth
  Than palaces of gold;

Better the blind faith of our youth
  Than doubt, which all truth braves;
Better to mourn, God's children dear,
  Than laugh, the devil's slaves.

O Robert, Robert, life is sweet,
  And love is boundless gain:
Yet if I mind of you, my heart
  Is stabb'd with sudden pain:

And as in peace this Christmas eve
  I close our quiet doors,
And kiss "good-night" on sleeping heads —
  Such bonnie curls, — like yours:

I fall upon my bended knees
  With sobs that choke each word; —
"*On those who err and are deceived*
  Have mercy, O good LORD!"

AT LAST.

Down, down like a pale leaf dropping
  Under an autumn sky,
My love dropp'd into my bosom
  Quietly, quietly.

There was not a ray of sunshine
  And not a sound in the air,
As she trembled into my bosom —
  My love, no longer fair.

All year round in her beauty
  She dwelt on the tree-top high:
She danced in the summer breezes,
  She laugh'd to the summer sky.

I lay so low in the grass-dews,
  She sat so high above,
She never wist of my longing,
  She never dream'd of my love.

But when winds laid bare her dwelling,
  And her heart could find no rest,
I call'd — and she flutter'd downward
  Into my faithful breast.

I know that my love is fading;
  I know I cannot fold
Her fragrance from the frost-blight,
  Her beauty from the mould:

But a little, little longer
  She shall contented lie,
And wither away in the sunshine
  Silently, silently.

Come when thou wilt, grim winter,
  My year is crown'd and blest
If when my love is dying
  She die upon my breast.

THE AURORA ON THE CLYDE.

September, 1850.

AH me, how heavily the night comes down,
    Heavily, heavily:
Fade the curved shores, the blue hills' serried throng,
The darkening waves we oar'd in light and song:
Joy melts from us as sunshine from the sky
    And Patience with sad eye
Takes up her staff and drops her wither'd crown.

Our small boat heaves upon the heaving river,
    Wearily, wearily:
The flickering shore-lights come and go by fits;
Towering 'twixt earth and heaven dusk silence sits,
Death at her feet; above, infinity;
    Between, slow drifting by,
Our tiny boat, like life, floats onward ever.

Pale, mournful hour, — too early night that falls
    Drearily, drearily,

Come not so soon! Return, return, bright day,
Kind voices, smiles, blue mountains, sunny bay!
In vain! Life's dial cannot backward fly:
    The dark time comes. Low lie,
And listen, soul. Oft in the night, God calls.

* * * * * *

Light, light on the black river! How it gleams,
    Solemnly, solemnly!
Like troops of pale ghosts on their pensive march,
Treading the far heavens in a luminous arch,
Each after each: phantasms serene and high
    From that eternity
Where all earth's sharpest woes grow dim as dreams.

Let us drink in the glory, full and whole,
    Silently, silently:
Gaze, till it lulls all pain, all vain desires:—
See now, that radiant bow of pillar'd fires
Spanning the hills like dawn, until they lie
    In soft tranquillity,
And all night's ghastly glooms asunder roll.

Look, look again! the vision changes fast,
    Gloriously, gloriously:
That was heaven's gate with its illumined road,
But this *is* heaven; the very throne of God
Hung with flame curtains of celestial dye

Waving perpetually,
While to and fro innumerous angels haste.

I see no more the stream, the boat that moves
Mournfully, mournfully :
And we who sit, poor prisoners of clay:
It is not night, it is immortal day,
Where the One Presence fills eternity,
And each, His servant high,
For ever praises and for ever loves.

O soul, forget the weight that drags thee down
Deathfully, deathfully:
Know thyself. As this glory wraps thee round,
Let it melt off the chains that long have bound
Thy strength. Stand free before thy God and cry—
"My Father, here am I:
Give to me as Thou wilt — first cross, then crown."

AN AURORA BOREALIS.

Roslin Castle.

O STRANGE soft gleam, O ghostly dawn
  That never brightens unto day;
Ere earth's mirk pale once more be drawn
  Let us look out beyond the grey.

It is just midnight by the clock —
  There is no sound on glen or hill,
The moaning linn adown its rock
  Leaps, but the woods lie dark and still.

Austere against the kindling sky
  Yon broken turret blacker grows;
Harsh light, to show remorselessly
  Ruins night hid in kind repose!

Nay, beauteous light, nay, light that fills
  The whole heaven like a dream of morn,
As waking upon northern hills
  She smiles to find herself new-born, —

Strange light, I know thou wilt not stay,
That many an hour must come and go
Before the pale November day
Break in the east, forlorn and slow.

Yet blest one gleam — one gleam like this,
When all heaven brightens in our sight,
And the long night that was and is
And shall be, vanishes in light:

O blest one hour like this! to rise
And see grief's shadows backward roll;
While bursts on unaccustomed eyes
The glad Aurora of the soul.

AT THE LINN-SIDE.

Roslin.

O LIVING, living water,
So busy and so bright,
Aye flashing in the morning beams,
And sounding through the night;
O golden-shining water —
Would God that I might be
A vocal message from His mouth
Into the world, like thee!

O merry, merry water,
Which nothing e'er affrays;
And as it pours from rock to rock
Nothing e'er stops or stays;
But past cool heathery hollows
And gloomy pools it flows;
Past crags that fain would shut it in
Leaps through — and on it goes.

O fresh'ning, sparkling water,
  O voice that 's never still,
Though winter lays her dead-white hand
  On brae and glen and hill;
Though no leaf 's left to flutter
  In woods all mute and hoar,
Yet thou, O river, night and day
  Thou runnest evermore.

No foul thing can pollute thee;
  Thy swiftness casts aside
All ill, like a good heart and true,
  However sorely tried.
O living, living water,
  So fresh and bright and free —
God lead us through this changeful world
  For ever pure, like thee!

A HYMN FOR CHRISTMAS MORNING.

1855.

It is the Christmas time:
And up and down twixt heaven and earth,
In glorious grief and solemn mirth,
The shining angels climb.

And unto everything
That lives and moves, for heaven, on earth,
With equal share of grief and mirth,
The shining angels sing:—

"Babes new-born, undefiled,
In lowly hut, or mansion wide—
Sleep safely through this Christmas-tide
When Jesus was a child.

"O young men, bold and free,
In peopled town, or desert grim,
When ye are tempted like to Him,
'The man Christ Jesus' see.

"Poor mothers, with your hoard
Of endless love and countless pain —
Remember all her grief, her gain,
The Mother of the Lord.

"Mourners, half blind with woe,
Look up! One standeth in this place,
And by the pity of His face
The Man of Sorrows know.

"Wanderers in far countrie,
O think of Him who came, forgot,
To His own, and they received Him not —
Jesus of Galilee.

"O all ye who have trod
The wine-press of affliction, lay
Your hearts before His heart this day —
Behold the Christ of God!"

A PSALM FOR NEW YEAR'S EVE.

1855.

A Friend stands at the door;
In either tight-closed hand
Hiding rich gifts, three hundred and three score:
Waiting to strew them daily o'er the land
Even as seed the sower.
Each drops he, treads it in and passes by:
It cannot be made fruitful till it die.

O good New Year, we clasp
This warm shut hand of thine,
Loosing for ever, with half sigh, half gasp,
That which from ours falls like dead fingers' twine:
Ay, whether fierce its grasp
Has been, or gentle, having been, we know
That it was blessed: let the Old Year go.

O New Year, teach us faith!
The road of life is hard:
When our feet bleed and scourging winds us scathe,
Point thou to Him whose visage was more marr'd

Than any man's: who saith
"Make straight paths for your feet" — and to the
opprest —
"Come ye to Me, and I will give you rest."

Yet hang some lamp-like hope
Above this unknown way,
Kind year, to give our spirits freer scope
And our hands strength to work while it is day.
But if that way must slope
Tombward, O bring before our fading eyes
The lamp of life, the Hope that never dies.

Comfort our souls with love, —
Love of all human kind;
Love special, close — in which like shelter'd dove
Each weary heart its own safe nest may find;
And love that turns above
Adoringly; contented to resign
All loves, if need be, for the Love Divine.

Friend, come thou like a friend,
And whether bright thy face,
Or dim with clouds we cannot comprehend, —
We'll hold out patient hands, each in his place,
And trust thee to the end.
Knowing thou leadest onwards to those spheres
Where there are neither days nor months nor years.

FAITHFUL IN VANITY-FAIR.

Suggested by one of David Scott's illustrations of "Pilgrim's Progress."

I.

THE great human whirlpool — 't is seething and seething:
On! No time for shrieking out — scarcely for breathing:
All toiling and moiling, some feebler, some bolder,
But each sees a fiend-face grim over his shoulder:
Thus merrily live they in Vanity-fair.

The great human caldron — it boils ever higher:
Some drowning, some sinking; while some, stealing nigher
Athirst, come and lean o'er its outermost verges,
Or touch, as a child's feet touch, timorous, the surges —
One plunge — lo! more souls swamp'd in Vanity-fair.

Let 's live while we live; for to-morrow all 's over:
Drink deep, drunkard bold; and kiss close, madden'd
lover;
Smile, hypocrite, smile; it is no such hard labour,
While each stealthy hand stabs the heart of his
neighbour —
Faugh! Fear not: we 've *no* hearts in Vanity-fair.

The mad crowd divides and then soon closes after:
Afar towers the pyre. Through the shouting and
laughter
"What new sport is this?" gasps a reveller, half
turning. —
"One Faithful, meek fool, who is led to the burn-
ing,
He cumber'd us sorely in Vanity-fair.

"A dreamer, who held every man for a brother;
A coward, who, smit on one cheek, gave the other;
A fool, whose blind soul took as truth all our lying,
Too simple to live, so best fitted for dying:
Sure, such are best swept out of Vanity-fair."

II.

SILENCE! though the flames arise and quiver:
Silence! though the crowd howls on for ever:
Silence! Through this fiery purgatory
God is leading up a soul to glory.

See, the white lips with no moans are trembling,
Hate of foes or plaint of friends' dissembling;
If sighs come — his patient prayers outlive them,
"*Lord — these know not what they do. Forgive them!*"

Thirstier still the roaring flames are glowing;
Fainter in his ear the laughter growing;
Brief will last the fierce and fiery trial,
Angel welcomes drown the earth denial.

Now the amorous death-fires, gleaming ruddy,
Clasp him close. Down drops the quivering body,
While through harmless flames ecstatic flying
Shoots the beauteous soul. This, this is *dying*.

Lo, the opening sky with splendour rifted,
Lo, the palm-branch for his hands uplifted:
Lo, the immortal chariot, cloud-descending,
And its legion'd angels close attending.

Let his poor dust mingle with the embers
While the crowds sweep on and none remembers:
Saints unnumber'd through the Infinite Glory,
Praising God, recount the martyr's story.

HER LIKENESS.

A GIRL, who has so many wilful ways
She would have caused Job's patience to forsake
him ;
Yet is so rich in all that 's girlhood's praise,
Did Job himself upon her goodness gaze,
A little better she would surely make him.

Yet is this girl I sing in nought uncommon,
And very far from angel yet, I trow.
Her faults, her sweetnesses, are purely human ;
Yet she 's more lovable as simple woman
Than any one diviner that I know.

Therefore I wish that she may safely keep
This womanhede, and change not, only grow ;
From maid to matron, youth to age, may creep,
And in perennial blessedness, still reap
On every hand of that which she doth sow.

ONLY A DREAM.

"I waked — she fled: and day brought back my night."

METHOUGHT I saw thee yesternight
  Sit by me in the olden guise,
The white robes and the palm foregone,
Weaving instead of amaranth crown
  A web of mortal dyes.

I cried, "Where hast thou been so long?"
  (The mild eyes turn'd and mutely smiled:)
"Why dwellest thou in far-off lands?
What is that web within thy hands?"
  — "I work for thee, my child."

I clasp'd thee in my arms and wept;
  I kiss'd thee oft with passion wild:
I pour'd fond questions, tender blame;
Still thy sole answer was the same, —
  "I work for thee, my child."

"Come and walk with me as of old."
  Then camest thou, silent as before;
We pass'd along that churchyard way
We used to tread each Sabbath day,
  Till one trod earth no more.

I felt thy hand upon my arm,
  Beside me thy meek face I saw,
Yet through the sweet familiar grace
A something spiritual could trace
  That left a nameless awe.

Trembling I said, "Long years have pass'd
  Since thou wert from my side beguiled;
Now thou 'rt return'd and all shall be
As was before." — Half-pensively
  Thou answered'st — "Nay, my child."

I pleaded sore: "Hadst thou forgot
  The love wherewith we loved of old, —
The long sweet days of converse blest,
The nights of slumber on thy breast, —
  Wert thou to me grown cold?"

There beam'd on me those eyes of heaven
  That wept no more, but ever smiled;
"Love only *is* love in that Home

Where I abide — where, till thou come,
  I work for thee, my child."

If from my sight thou passedst then,
  Or if my sobs the dream exiled,
I know not: but in memory clear
I seem these strange words still to hear,
  "*I work for thee, my child.*"

TO MY GODCHILD ALICE.

Alice, Alice, little Alice,
My new-christen'd baby Alice,
  Can there ever rhymes be found
To express my wishes for thee
In a silvery flowing, worthy
  Of that silvery sound?
Bonnie Alice, Lady Alice,
  Sure, this sweetest name must be
A true omen to thee, Alice,
  Of a life's long melody.

Alice, Alice, little Alice,
Mayst thou prove a golden chalice,
  Fill'd with holiness like wine:
With rich blessings running o'er
Yet replenish'd evermore
  From a fount divine:
Alice, Alice, little Alice,
  When this future comes to thee,

In thy young life's brimming chalice
  Keep some drops of balm for me!

Alice, Alice, little Alice,
Mayst thou grow a goodly palace,
  Fitly framed from roof to floors,
Pure unto the inmost centre,
While high thoughts like angels enter
  At the open doors:
Alice, Alice, little Alice,
  When this beauteous sight I see,
In thy woman-heart's wide palace
  Keep one nook of love for me.

Alice, Alice, little Alice, —
Sure the verse halts out of malice
  To the thoughts it feebly bears,
And thy name's soft echoes, ranging
From quaint rhyme to rhyme, are changing
  Into silent prayers.
God be with thee, little Alice,
  Of His bounteousness may He
Fill the chalice, build the palace,
  Here, unto eternity!

EIGHTEEN SONNETS.

RESIGNING.

"Poor heart, what bitter words we speak
When God speaks of resigning!"

CHILDREN, that lay their pretty garlands by
So piteously, yet with a humble mind;
Sailors, who, when their ship rocks in the wind,
Cast out her freight with half-averted eye,
Riches for life exchanging solemnly,
Lest they should never gain the wish'd-for shore;—
Thus we, O Father, standing Thee before,
Do lay down at Thy feet without a sigh
Each after each our precious things and rare,
Our dear heart-jewels and our garlands fair.
Perhaps Thou knewest that the flowers would die,
And the long-voyaged hoards be found but dust:
So took'st them, while unchanged. To Thee we trust
For incorruptible treasure: Thou art just.

SAINT ELIZABETH OF BOHEMIA.

Would that we two were lying
  Beneath the churchyard sod,
With our limbs at rest in the green earth's breast,
  And our souls at home with God.

KINGSLEY'S *Saint's Tragedy.*

I.

I NEVER lay me down to sleep at night
But in my heart I sing that little song:
The angels hear it as, a pitying throng,
They touch my burning lids with fingers bright
As moonbeams, pale, impalpable, and light:
And when my daily pious tasks are done,
And all my patient prayers said one by one,
God hears it. Seems it sinful in His sight
That round my slow burnt-offering of quench'd will
One quivering human sigh creeps wind-like still?
That when my orisons celestial fail
Rises one note of natural human wail?
Dear lord, spouse, hero, martyr, saint! ere long,
I trust, God will forgive my singing that poor song.

II.

A YEAR ago I bade my little son
Bear upon pilgrimage a heavy load
Of alms ; he cried, half-fainting on the road,
" Mother, oh mother, would the day were done ! "
Him I reproved with tears, and said " Go on !
Nor pause nor murmur till thy task be o'er." —
Would not God say to me the same, and more ?
I will not sing that song. Thou, dearest one,
Husband — no, brother ! — stretch thy stedfast hand
And let mine grasp it. Now, I also stand,
My woman weakness nerved to strength like thine ;
We 'll quaff life's aloe-cup as if 't were wine
Each to the other ; journeying on apart,
Till at heaven's golden doors we two leap heart to
heart.

A MARRIAGE-TABLE.

W. H. L. and F. R.

THERE was a marriage-table where One sate,
Haply, unnoticed, till they craved His aid:
Thenceforward does it seem that He has made
All virtuous marriage-tables consecrate:
And so, at this, where without pomp or state
We sit, and only say, or mute, are fain
To wish the simple words "God bless these twain!"
I think that He who "in the midst" doth wait
Oft-times, would not abjure our prayerful cheer,
But, as at Cana, list with gracious ear
To us, beseeching, that the Love divine
May ever at their household table sit,
Make all His servants who encompass it,
And change life's bitterest waters into wine.

MICHAEL THE ARCHANGEL.

A Statuette.

I.

My white archangel, with thy stedfast eyes
Beholding all this empty ghost-fill'd room,
Thy clasp'd hands resting on the sword of doom,
Thy firm, close lips, not made for human sighs
Or smiles, or kisses sweet, or bitter cries,
But for divine exhorting, holy song
And righteous counsel, bold from seraph tongue.
Beautiful angel, strong as thou art wise,
Would that the sight of thee made wise and strong!
Would that this sheathèd sword of thine, which lies
Stonily idle, could gleam out among
The spiritual hosts of enemies
That tempting shriek — "Requite thou wrong with
wrong."
Lama Sabachthani — How long, how long.

II.

Michael, the leader of the hosts of God,
Who warr'd with Satan for the body of him
Whom, living, God had loved — If cherubim
With cherubim contended for one clod
Of human dust, for forty years that trod
The gloomy desert of heaven's chastisement,
Are there not ministering angels sent
To battle with the devils that roam abroad,
Clutching our living souls? "The living, still
The living, they shall praise Thee!" — Let some great
Invisible spirit enter in and fill
The howling chambers of hearts desolate;
With looks like thine, O Michael, strong and wise,
My white archangel with the stedfast eyes.

I.

BEATRICE TO DANTE.

"Guardami ben. Ben son, ben son." *

REGARD me well: I am thy love, thy love;
Thy blessing, thy delight, thy hope, thy peace:
Thy joy above all joys that break and cease
When their full waves in widest circles move:
Thy bird of comfort, thine eternal dove,
Whom thou did send out of thy mournful breast
To flutter back and point thee to thy rest:
Thine angel, who forgets her crown star-wove
To come to thee with folded woman-hands
Pleading — "Look on me, Beatrice, who stands
Before thee; by the Triune Light divine
Undazzled, still beholds thy human face,
And is more happy in this happy place
That thou alone art hers and she is thine."

* Suggested by a statue of Beatrice, bearing this motto.

II.

DANTE TO BEATRICE.

I SEE thee, gliding towards me with slow pace
Across the azure fields of Paradise,
Where thine each footstep makes a star arise.
So from this heart's once void but infinite space
Each strange sweet touch of thy celestial grace
In the old mortal life, struck out some spark
To light the world, though all my heaven lay dark.
O Beatrice, cypresses enlace
My laurels: none have grown save tear-bedew'd —
Salt tears that sank into the earth unview'd,
And sprang up green to form a crown of bays.
Take it! At thy dear feet I lay my all,
What men my honours, virtues, glories, call:
I lived, loved, suffer'd, sung — for thy sole praise.

A QUESTION.

I.

Soul, spirit, genius — which thou art — that whence
I know not, rose upon this mortal frame
Like the sun o'er the mountains, all aflame,
Seen large through mists of childish innocence,
And year by year with me uptravelling thence,
As hour by hour the day-star, madest aspire
My nature, interpenetrate with fire
It felt but understood not — strong, intense,
Wisdom with folly mix'd, and gold with clay; —
Soul, thou hast journey'd with me all this way.
Oft hidden and o'erclouded, oft array'd
In scorching splendours that my earth-life burn'd,
Yet ever unto thee my true life turn'd,
For, dim or clear, 't was thou my day-light made.

II.

Soul, dwelling oft in God's infinitude,
And sometimes seeming no more part of me —

This *me*, worms' heritage — than that sun can be
Part of the earth he has with warmth imbued, —
Whence camest thou? whither goest thou? I, sub-
dued
With awe of mine own being — thus sit still,
Dumb, on the summit of this lonely hill,
Whose dry November-grasses dew-bestrewed
Mirror a million suns — That sun, so bright,
Passes, as thou must pass, Soul, into night:
Art thou afraid, who solitary hast trod
A path I know not, from a source to a bourne,
Both which I know not? fear'st thou to return
Alone, even as thou camest, *alone*, to God?

ANGEL FACES.

"And with the dawn those angel faces smile
That I have loved long since, and lost awhile."

I.

I SHALL not paint them. God them sees, and I:
No other can, nor need. They have no form,
I may not close with human kisses warm
Their eyes which shine afar or from on high,
But never will shine nearer till I die.
How long, how long! See, I am growing old;
I have quite ceased to note in my hair's fold
The silver threads that there in ambush lie;
Some angel faces bent from heaven would pine
To trace the sharp lines graven upon mine;
What matter? in the wrinkles plough'd by care
Let age tread after, sowing immortal seeds;
All this life's harvest yielded, wheat or weeds,
Is reap'd, methinks: at last my little field lies bare.

II.

But in the night time, 'twixt it and the stars,
The angel faces still come glimmering by;
No death-pale shadow, no averted eye
Marking the inevitable doom that bars
Me from them. Not a cloud their aspect mars;
And my sick spirit walks with them hand in hand
By the cool waters of a pleasant land:
Sings with them o'er again, without its jars,
The psalm of life, that ceased as one by one
Their voices dropping off, left mine alone
With dull monotonous wail to grieve the air, —
O solitary love, that art so strong,
I think God will have pity on thee ere long,
And take thee where thou 'lt find those angel faces
fair.

SUNDAY MORNING BELLS.

From the near city comes the clang of bells:
Their hundred jarring diverse tones combine
In one faint misty harmony, as fine
As the soft note yon winter robin swells.—
What if to Thee in Thine Infinity
These multiform and many-colour'd creeds
Seem but the robe man wraps as masquers' weeds
Round the one living truth Thou givest him—Thee?
What if these varied forms that worship prove,
Being heart-worship, reach Thy perfect ear
But as a monotone, complete and clear,
Of which the music is, through Christ's name, Love?
For ever rising in sublime increase
To "Glory in the Highest—on earth peace?"

CŒUR DE LION:

Marochetti's Statue in the Great Exhibition of 1851.

I.

RICHARD THE LION-HEARTED, crown'd serene
With the true royalty of perfect man;
Seated in stone above the praise or ban
Of these mix'd crowds who come and gaping lean
As if to see what the word "king" might mean
In those old times. Behold! what need that rim
Of crown 'gainst this blue sky, to signal him
A monarch, of the monarchs that have been
And, perhaps, are not? — Read his destinies
In the full brow o'er-arching kingly eyes,
In the strong hands, grasping both rein and sword,
In the close mouth, so sternly beautiful: —
Surely, a man who his own spirit can rule;
Lord of himself, therefore his brethren's lord.

II.

"*O Richard, O mon roi.*" So minstrels sigh'd.
The many-centuried voice dies fast away
Amidst the turmoil of our modern day.
How know we but these green-wreath'd legends hide
An ugly truth that never could abide
In this our living world's far purer air?—
Nevertheless, O statue, rest thou there,
Our Richard, of all chivalry the pride;
Or if not the true Richard, still a type
Of the old regal glory, fallen, o'er-ripe,
And giving place to better blossoming:
Stand—imaging the grand heroic days;
And let our little children come and gaze,
Whispering with innocent awe—"This *was* a King."

GUNS OF PEACE.

Sunday Night, March 30th, 1856.

GHOSTS of dead soldiers in the battle slain,
Ghosts of dead heroes dying nobler far
In the long patience of inglorious war,
Of famine, cold, heat, pestilence, and pain, —
All ye whose loss makes our victorious gain —
This quiet night, as sounds the cannon's tongue,
Do ye look down the trembling stars among
Viewing our peace and war with like disdain?
Or wiser grown since reaching those new spheres,
Smile ye on those poor bones ye sow'd as seed
For this our harvest, nor regret the deed? —
Yet lift one cry with us to Heavenly ears —
"Strike with Thy bolt the next red flag unfurl'd,
And make all wars to cease throughout the world."

DAVID'S CHILD.

—"Is the child dead?"—And they said, "He is dead."

In face of a great sorrow like to death
How do we wrestle night and day with tears;
How do we fast and pray; how small appears
The outside world, while, hanging on some breath
Of fragile hope, the chamber where we lie
Includes all space.—But if sudden at last
The blow falls; or by incredulity
Fond led, we—never having one thought cast
Towards years where "the child" was not—see it die,
And with it all our future, all our past,—
We just look round us with a dull surprise:
For lesser pangs we had fill'd earth with cries
Of wild and angry grief that would be heard:—
But when the heart is broken—not a word.

A WORD IN SEASON.

"This is a day the Lord hath made." — Thus spake
The good religious heart, unstain'd, unworn,
Watching the golden glory of the morn. —
Since, on each happy day that came to break
Like sunlight o'er this silent life of mine,
Yea, on each beauteous morning I saw shine,
I have remember'd these your words, rejoiced
And been glad in it. So, o'er many-voiced
Tumultuous harmonies of tropic seas,
Which chant an everlasting farewell grand
Between ourselves and you and the old land,
Receive this token: many words chance-sown
May oftentimes have taken root and grown,
To bear good fruit perennially, like these.

THE PATH THROUGH THE SNOW.

BARE and sunshiny, bright and bleak,
Rounded cold as a dead maid's cheek,
Folded white as a sinner's shroud,
Or wandering angel's robes of cloud. —
Well I know, well I know
Over the fields the path through the snow.

Narrow and rough it lies between
Wastes where the wind sweeps, biting keen:
Every step of the slippery road
Marks where some weary foot has trod;
Who 'll go, who 'll go
After the rest on the path through the snow?

They who would tread it must walk alone,
Silent and stedfast — one by one:
Dearest to dearest can only say,
"My heart! I 'll follow thee all the way,
As we go, as we go,
Each after each on this path through the snow."

It may be under that western haze
Lurks the omen of brighter days;
That each sentinel tree is quivering
Deep at its core with the sap of spring,
And while we go, while we go,
Green grass-blades pierce through the glittering snow.

It may be the unknown path will tend
Never to any earthly end,
Die with the dying day obscure,
And never lead to a human door:
That none know who did go
Patiently once on this path through the snow.

No matter, no matter! the path shines plain;
These pure snow-crystals will deaden pain;
Above, like stars in the deep blue dark,
Eyes that love us look down and mark.
Let us go, let us go,
Whither heaven leads in the path through the snow.

THE PATH THROUGH THE CORN.

Wavy and bright in the summer air,
Like a pleasant sea when the wind blows fair,
And its roughest breath has scarcely curled
The green highway to a distant world, —
Soft whispers passing from shore to shore,
As from hearts content, yet desiring more —
Who feels forlorn,
Wandering thus down the path through the corn?

A short space since, and the dead leaves lay
Mouldering under the hedgerow grey,
Nor hum of insect, nor voice of bird,
O'er the desolate field was ever heard;
Only at eve the pallid snow
Blushed rose-red in the red sun-glow;
Till, one blest morn,
Shot up into life the young green corn.

Small and feeble, slender and pale,
It bent its head to the winter gale,

Hearkened the wren's soft note of cheer,
Hardly believing spring was near:
Saw chestnuts bud out and campions blow,
And daisies mimic the vanished snow
        Where it was born,
On either side of the path through the corn.

The corn, the corn, the beautiful corn,
Rising wonderful, morn by morn:
First, scarce as high as a fairy's wand,
Then, just in reach of a child's wee hand;
Then growing, growing, tall, brave, and strong:
With the voice of new harvests in its song;
        While in fond scorn
The lark out-carols the whispering corn.

A strange, sweet path, formed day by day,
How, when, and wherefore, we cannot say,
No more than of our life-paths we know,
Whither they lead us, why we go;
Or whether our eyes shall ever see
The wheat in the ear or the fruit on the tree;
        Yet, who 's forlorn?—
He who watered the furrows can ripen the corn.

THE GOOD OF IT.

A Cynic's Song.

Some men strut proudly, all purple and gold,
  Hiding queer deeds 'neath a cloak of good fame;
I creep along, braving hunger and cold,
  To keep my heart stainless as well as my name;
    So, so, where is the good of it?

Some clothe bare Truth in fine garments of words,
  Fetter her free limbs with cumbersome state:
With me, let me sit at the lordliest boards,
  "I love" means *I love*, and "I hate" means *I hate*,
    But, but, where is the good of it?

Some have rich dainties and costly attire,
  Guests fluttering round them and duns at the door:
I crouch alone at my plain board and fire,
  Enjoy what I pay for and scorn to have more.
    Yet, yet, where is the good of it?

Some gather round them a phalanx of friends,
  Scattering affection like coin in a crowd;
I keep my heart for the few that heaven sends,
  Where they'll find their names writ when I lie in
      my shroud.
    Still, still, where is the good of it?

Some toy with love, lightly come, lightly go,
  A blithe game at hearts, little worth, little cost:—
I staked my whole soul on one desperate throw,
  A life 'gainst an hour's sport. We played; and
      I—lost.
    Ha, ha, such was the good of it!

MORAL: ADDED ON HIS DEATH-BED.

Turn the Past's mirror backward. Its shadows removed,
  The dim confused mass becomes softened, sublime:
I have worked—I have felt—I have lived—I
      have loved,
  And each was a step towards the goal I now
      climb:
    Thou, God, Thou sawest the good of it.

MINE.

For a German Air.

O HOW my heart is beating as her name I keep
repeating,
And I drink up joy like wine:
O how my heart is beating as her name I keep
repeating,
For the lovely girl is mine!
She 's rich, she 's fair, beyond compare,
Of noble mind, serene and kind —
And how my heart is beating as her name I keep
repeating,
For the lovely girl is mine!

O how my heart is beating as her name I keep
repeating,
In a music soft and fine;
O how my heart is beating as her name I keep
repeating,
For the girl I love is mine.

She owns no lands, has no white hands,
Her lot is poor, her life obscure; —
Yet how my heart is beating as her name I keep
repeating,
For the girl I love is mine!

A GHOST AT THE DANCING.

A WIND-SWEPT tulip-bed — a colour'd cloud
Of butterflies careering in the air —
A many-figured arras stirred to life,
And merry unto midnight music dumb —
So the dance whirls. Do any think of thee,
Amiel, Amiel?

Friends greet each other — countless rills of talk
Meander round, scattering a spray of smiles.
Surely — the news was false. One minute more,
And thou wilt stand here, tall and quiet-eyed,
Shaksperian beauty in thy pensive face,
Amiel, Amiel.

Many here knew and loved thee — I nor loved,
Scarce knew — yet in thy place a shadow glides,
And a face shapes itself from empty air,
Watching the dancers, grave and quiet-eyed —

Eyes that now see the angels evermore,
    Amiel, Amiel.

On just such night as this, 'midst dance and song,
I bade thee carelessly a light good-bye —
" Good-bye " — saidst thou ; " A happy journey
        home ! "
Was the unseen death-angel at thy side,
Mocking those words — " *A happy journey home,*"
    Amiel, Amiel ?

Ay, we play fool's play still ; thou hast gone home.
While these dance here, a mile hence o'er thy
        grave
Drifts the deep New Year snow. The wondrous
        gate
We spoke of, thou hast enter'd ; I without
Grope ignorant still — thou dost its secrets know,
    Amiel, Amiel.

What if, thus sitting where we sat last year,
Thou camest, took'st up our broken thread of talk,
And told'st of that new Home, which far I view,
As children, wandering on through wintry fields,
Mark on the hill the father's window shine,
    Amiel, Amiel ?

No. We shall see thy pleasant face no more;
Thy words on earth are ended. Yet thou livest;
'T is we who die. — I too, one day shall come,
And, unseen, watch these shadows, quiet-eyed —
Then flit back to thy land, the living land,
    Amiel, Amiel.

MY CHRISTIAN NAME.

My Christian name, my Christian name,
 I never hear it now:
None have the right to utter it,
 'T is lost, I scarce know how.
My worldly name the world speaks loud;
 Thank God for well-earned fame!
But silence sits at my cold hearth, —
 I have no household name.

My Christian name, my Christian name,
 It has an uncouth sound;
My mother chose it out of those
 In Bible pages found:
Mother, whose accents made half sweet
 What else I held in shame,
Dost thou remember up in heaven
 My poor lost Christian name?

Brothers and sisters, mockers oft
 Of the quaint name I bore,

Would I could leap back years, to hear
  Ye shout it out once more!
One speaks it still, in written lines,
  The last fraternal claim:
But the wide seas between us drown
  Its sound — my Christian name.

I had a long dream once. *Her* voice
  Might breathe the homely word,
And make it music — as love makes
  Any name, said or heard.
O, dumb, dumb lips! — O, silent heart!
  Though it is no one's blame:
Now while I live I 'll never hear
  Her speak my Christian name.

God send her bliss, and send me rest!
  If her white footsteps calm
Should track my bleeding feet, God make
  To them each blood-drop balm!
Peace — peace. O mother, put thou forth
  Thine elder holier claim,
And the first word I hear in heaven
  May be my Christian name.

A DEAD BABY.

LITTLE soul, for such brief space that entered
  In this little body straight and chilly,
Little life that fluttered and departed,
  Like a moth from an unopened lily,
Little being, without name or nation,
Where is now thy place among creation?

Little dark-lashed eyes, unclosèd never,
  Little mouth, by earthly food ne'er tainted,
Little breast, that just once heaved, and settled
  In eternal slumber, white and sainted, —
Child, shall I in future children's faces
See some pretty look that thine re-traces?

Is this thrill that strikes across my heart-strings
  And in dew beneath my eyelid gathers,
Token of the bliss thou mightst have brought me,
  Dawning of the love they call a father's?
Do I hear through this still room a sighing
Like thy spirit to me its author crying?

Whence didst come and whither take thy journey,
  Little soul, of me and mine created?
Must thou lose us, and we thee, for ever,
  O strange life, by minutes only dated?
Or new flesh assuming, just to prove us,
In some other babe return and love us?

Idle questions all: yet our beginning
  Like our ending, rests with the Life-sender,
With whom nought is lost, and nought spent vainly:
  Unto Him this little one I render.
Hide the face — the tiny coffin cover:
So, our first dream, our first hope — is over.

FOR MUSIC.

Along the shore, along the shore
  I see the wavelets meeting:
But thee I see—ah, never more,
  For all my wild heart's beating.
The little wavelets come and go,
The tide of life ebbs to and fro,
  Advancing and retreating:
But from the shore, the stedfast shore,
  The sea is parted never:
And mine I hold thee evermore,
  For ever and for ever.

Along the shore, along the shore,
  I hear the waves resounding,
But thou wilt cross them never more
  For all my wild heart's bounding:
The moon comes out above the tide
And quiets all the billows wide
  Her pathway bright surrounding:

Thus on the shore, the dreary shore,
  I walk with weak endeavour;
I have thy love's light evermore,
  For ever and for ever.

THE CANARY IN HIS CAGE.

SING away, ay, sing away,
  Merry little bird,
Always gayest of the gay,
Though a woodland roundelay
  You ne'er sung nor heard;
Though your life from youth to age
Passes in a narrow cage.

Near the window wild birds fly,
  Trees are waving round:
Fair things everywhere you spy
Through the glass pane's mystery,
  Your small life's small bound:
Nothing hinders your desire
But a little gilded wire.

Like a human soul you seem
  Shut in golden bars:
Placed amidst earth's sunshine-stream,
Singing to the morning beam,

Dreaming 'neath the stars;
Seeing all life's pleasures clear, —
But they never can come near.

Never! Sing, bird-poet mine,
As most poets do; —
Guessing by an instinct fine
At some happiness divine
Which they never knew.
Lonely in a prison bright
Hymning for the world's delight.

Yet, my birdie, you 're content
In your tiny cage:
Not a carol thence is sent
But for happiness is meant —
Wisdom pure as sage:
Teaching, the true poet's part
Is to sing with merry heart.

So, lie down thou peevish pen,
Eyes, shake off all tears;
And my wee bird, sing again:
I 'll translate your song to men
In these future years.
"Howsoe'er thy lot 's assign'd,
Bear it with a cheerful mind."

CONSTANCY IN INCONSTANCY.

AN OLD MAN'S CONFESSION.

She has a large still heart — this lady of mine,
(Not mine, i' faith! nor would I that she were:)
She walks this world of ours like Grecian nymph,
Pure with a marble pureness, moving on
Among the herd of men, environ'd round
With native airs of deep Olympian calm.
I have a great love for that lady of mine:
I like to watch her motions, trick of face,
And turn of thought, when speaking high and wise
The tongue of gods, not men. Ay, every day,
And twenty times a day, I start to catch
Some look or gesture of familiar mould,
And then my panting soul leans forth to her
Like some sick traveller who astonied sees
Gliding across the distant twilight fields —
His lovely, lost, beloved memory-fields —
The shadowy people of an earlier world.

I have a friend, how dearly liked, heart-warm,
Did I confess, sure she and all would smile:
I watch her as she steals in some dull room
That brightens at her entrance — slow lets fall
A word or two of wise simplicity,
Then goes, and at her going all seems dark.
Little she knows this: little thinks each brow
Lightens, each heart grows purer with her eyes,
Good, honest eyes — clear, upward, righteous eyes,
That look as if they saw the dim unseen,
And learnt from thence their deep compassionate calm.
Why do I precious hold this friend of mine?
Why in our talks, our quiet fireside talks,
When we, two earnest travellers through the dark,
Grasp at the guiding threads that homeward lead,
Seems its another soul than hers looks out
From these her eyes? — until I oft-times start
And quiver, as when some soft ignorant hand
Touches the barb hid in a long-heal'd wound.
Yet still no blame, but thanks to thee, dear friend,
Ay, even when we wander back at eve,
Thy careless arm loose link'd within my own —
The same height as I gaze down — nay, the hair
Her very colour — fluttering 'neath the stars —
The same large stars which lit that earlier world.

I have another love — whose dewy looks
Are fresh with life's young dawn. I prophesy
The streak of light now trembling on the hills
Will broaden out into a glorious day.
Thou sweet one, meek as good, and good as fair,
Wise as a woman, harmless as a child,
I love thee well! And yet not thee, not thee,
God knows — *they* know who sit among the stars.
As one whose sun was darken'd before noon,
Creeps patiently along the twilight lands,
Sees glow-worms, meteors, or tapers kind
Of an hour's burning, stops awhile to mark,
Thanks heaven for them, but never calls them day —
So love I these, and more. Yet thou, my sun,
Who rose, leap'd to thy zenith, sat there throned,
And made the whole earth day — look, if thou canst,
Out of thy veilèd glory, and behold
How all these lesser lights but come and go,
Mere reflexes of thee. Be it so! I keep
My face unto the eastward, where thou stand'st —
I *know* thou stand'st — behind the purpling hills,
And I shall wake and find morn in the world.

BURIED TO-DAY.

February 23, 1858.

BURIED to-day.
    When the soft green buds are bursting out,
    And up on the south wind comes a shout
Of village boys and girls at play
In the mild spring evening grey.

Taken away
    Sturdy of heart and stout of limb,
    From eyes that drew half their light from him,
And put low, low, underneath the clay,
In his spring — on this spring day.

Passes away
    All the pride of boy-life begun,
    All the hope of life yet to run;
Who dares to question when One saith "Nay."
Murmur not — only pray.

Enters to-day
    Another body in churchyard sod,
    Another soul on the life in God.
HIS Christ was buried — and lives alway:
Trust Him, and go your way.

THE MILL.

For an Irish Tune.

WINDING and grinding
 Round goes the mill:
Winding and grinding
 Should never stand still.
Ask not if neighbour
 Grind great or small:
Spare not *your* labour,
 Grind *your* wheat all.
Winding and grinding round goes the mill:
Winding and grinding should never stand still.

Winding and grinding
 Work through the day,
Grief never minding—
 Grind it away!
What though tears dropping
 Rust as they fall?

Have no wheel stopping —
Work comforts all.
Winding and grinding round goes the mill:
Winding and grinding should never stand still.

NORTH WIND.

Loud wind, strong wind, sweeping o'er the mountains,
Fresh wind, free wind, blowing from the sea,
Pour forth thy vials like streams from airy fountains,
Draughts of life to me.

Clear wind, cold wind, like a Northern giant,
Stars brightly threading thy cloud-driven hair,
Thrilling the blank night with thy voice defiant,
Lo! I meet thee there.

Wild wind, bold wind, like a strong-arm'd angel,
Clasp me and kiss me with thy kisses divine;
Breathe in this dull'd ear thy secret sweet evangel —
Mine — and only mine.

Fierce wind, mad wind, howling o'er the nations,
Knew'st thou how leapeth my heart as thou goest by:
Ah, thou wouldst pause awhile in a sudden patience
Like a human sigh.

Sharp wind, keen wind, cutting as word-arrows,
Empty thy quiverful! pass by! What is 't to thee,
That in some mortal eyes life's whole bright circle narrows,
To one misery?

Loud wind, strong wind, stay thou in the mountains,
Fresh wind, free wind, trouble not the sea.
Or lay thy deathly hand upon my heart's warm fountains,
That I hear not thee.

NOW AND AFTERWARDS.

"Two hands upon the breast and labour is past."
RUSSIAN PROVERB.

"Two hands upon the breast,
And labour 's done;
Two pale feet cross'd in rest —
The race is won;
Two eyes with coin-weights shut,
And all tears cease;
Two lips where grief is mute,
Anger at peace;" —
So pray we oftentimes, mourning our lot:
God in his kindness answereth not.

"Two hands to work addrest
Aye for His praise;
Two feet that never rest
Walking His ways;
Two eyes that look above
Through all their tears;

Two lips still breathing love,
  Not wrath, nor fears;"
So pray we afterwards, low on our knees;
Pardon those erring prayers! Father, hear these!

A SKETCH.

> "Emelie, that fayrer was to seene
>   Than is the lilye on hys stalke grene."—
> "Uprose the sun and uprose Emelie."

Dost thou thus love me, O thou beautiful?
So beautiful, that by thy side I seem
Like a great dusky cloud beside a star:
Yet thou creep'st o'er its edges, and it rests
On its lone path, the slow deep-hearted cloud —
Then opes a rift and lets thee enter in;
And with thy beauty shining on its breast,
Feels no more its own blackness — *thou* art fair.

Dost thou thus love me, O thou all beloved,
In whose large store the very meanest coin
Would out-buy my whole wealth? Yet here thou
        comest
Like a kind heiress from her purple and down
Uprising, who for pity cannot sleep,
But goes forth to the stranger at her gate —
The beggar'd stranger at her beauteous gate —
And clothes and feeds; scarce blest till she has blest.

Dost thou thus love me, O thou pure of heart,
Whose very looks are prayers? What could'st thou
see
In this forsaken pool by the yew-wood's side,
To sit down at its bank, and dip thy hand,
Saying, "It is so clear!" — And lo, ere long
Its blackness caught the shimmer of thy wings
Its slimes slid downward from thy stainless palm,
Its depths grew still that there thy form might rise.

O beautiful! O well-beloved! O rich
In all that makes my need! I lay me down
I' the shadow of thy love, and feel no pain.
The cloud floats on, thee glittering on its breast,
The beggar wears thy purple as his own:
The noisome waves, made calm, creep to thy feet
Rejoicing that they yet can image thee,
And beyond thee, God's heaven, thick-sown with
stars.

THE UNKNOWN COUNTRY.

To a German Air.

"Where is the unknown country?"
  I whisper'd sad and slow—
"The strange and awful country
  To which I soon must go, must go,
  To which I soon must go?"

Out of the unknown country
  A voice sang soft and low.
"O pleasant is that country
  And sweet it is to go, to go,
  And sweet it is to go.

"Along the shining country
  The peaceful rivers flow:
And in that wondrous country
  The tree of life does grow, does grow,
  The tree of life does grow."

Ah, then into that country
  Of which I nothing know,
The everlasting country,
  With willing heart I go, I go,
  With willing heart I go.

A CHILD'S SMILE.

"For I say unto you, that in heaven their angels do always behold the face of my Father which is in Heaven."

A CHILD'S smile — nothing more;
Quiet, and soft, and grave, and seldom seen;
Like summer lightning o'er,
Leaving the little face again serene.

I think, boy well-beloved,
Thine angel, who did grieve to see how far
Thy childhood is removed
From sports that dear to other children are,

On this pale cheek has thrown
The brightness of his countenance, and made
A beauty like his own —
That while we see it, we are half afraid,

And marvel, will it stay?
Or, long ere manhood, will that angel fair

Departing some sad day,
Steal the child-smile and leave the shadow care?

Nay, fear not. As is given
Unto this child the father watching o'er,
His angel up in heaven
Beholds Our Father's face for evermore.

And he will help him bear
His burthen, as his father helps him now;
So may he come to wear
That happy child-smile on an old man's brow.

VIOLETS.

SENT IN A LITTLE BOX.

Let them lie, yes, let them lie,
  They 'll be dead to-morrow:
Lift the lid up quietly
As you 'd lift the mystery
  Of a shrouded sorrow.

Let them lie, the fragrant things,
  Their sweet souls thus giving:
Let no breezes' ambient wings,
And no useless water-springs
  Lure them into living.

They have lived — they live no more:
  Nothing can requite them
For the gentle life they bore
And up-yielded in full-store
  While it did delight them.

Yet, poor flowers, not sad to die
  In the hand that slew ye,
Did ye leave the open sky,
And the winds that wander'd by,
  And the bees that knew ye.

Giving up a small earth place,
  And a day of blooming,
Here to lie in narrow space,
Smiling in this sickly face,
  This dull air perfuming?

O my pretty violets dead,
  Coffin'd from all gazes,
We will also smiling shed
Out of our flowers witherèd,
  Perfume of sweet praises.

And as ye, for this poor sake,
  Love with life are buying,
So, I doubt not, ONE will make
All our gather'd flowers to take
  Richer scent through dying.

EDENLAND.

For Music.

You remember where in starlight
  We two wander'd hand in hand,
While the night-flowers pour'd their perfume,
  And night-airs the still earth fann'd? —
There I, walking yester even,
  Felt like a ghost in Edenland.

I remember all you told me,
  Looking up as we did stand,
While my heart poured out its perfume,
  Like the night-flowers, in your hand;
And the path where we two wander'd
  Seem'd not like earth but Edenland.

Now the stars shine paler, colder
  Night-flowers die without your hand;
Yet my spirit walks beside you
  Everywhere, unsought, unbann'd.
And I wait till we shall wander
  Under the stars of Edenland.

THE HOUSE OF CLAY.

THERE was a house, a house of clay,
Wherein the inmate sat all day,
Merry and poor;
For Hope sat with her, heart to heart,
Fond and kind, fond and kind,
Vowing he never would depart, —
Till all at once he changed his mind:
"Sweetheart, good-bye!" He slipp'd away
And shut the door.

But Love came past, and looking in
With smile that pierced like sunbeam thin
Through wall, roof, floor,
Stood in the midst of that poor room,
Grand and fair, grand and fair,
Making a glory out of gloom: —
Till at the window mock'd grim Care:
Love sighed; "All lose, and nothing win?" —
He shut the door.

Then o'er the close-barr'd house of clay
Kind clematis and woodbine gay
    Crept more and more;
And bees humm'd merrily outside
    Loud and strong, loud and strong,
The inner silentness to hide,
    The patient silence all day long;
Till evening touch'd with finger grey
    The bolted door.

Most like, the next step passing by
Will be the Angel's, whose calm eye
    Marks rich, marks poor:
Who, fearing not, at any gate
    Stands and calls, stands and calls;
At which the inmate opens straight,—
    Whom, ere the crumbling clay-house falls,
He takes in kind arms silently,
    And shuts the door.

WINTER MOONLIGHT.

LOUD-VOICED night, with the wild wind blowing
    Many a tune;
Stormy night, with white rain-clouds going
    Over the moon;
Mystic night, that each minute changes,
Now as blue as the mountain-ranges
    Far, far away;
Now as black as a heart where strange is
    Joy, night or day.

Wondrous moonlight, unlike all moonlights
    Since I was born;
That on a hundred, bright as noonlights,
    Looks in slow scorn, —
Moonlights where the old vine-leaves quiver,
Moonlights shining on vale and river,
    Where old paths lie;
Moonlights — Night, blot their like for ever
    Out of the sky!

Hail, new moonlight, fierce, wild, and stormy,
    Wintry and bold!
Hail, sharp wind, that can strengthen, warm me,
    If ne'er so cold!
Not chance driven this deluge rages,
ONE doth pour out and ONE assuages;
    Under His hand
Drifting, Noah-like, into the ages,
    I shall touch land.

THE PLANTING.

"I said to my little son, who was watching tearfully a tree he had planted —'Let it alone: it will grow while you are sleeping.'"

PLANT it safe and sure, my child,
Then cease watching and cease weeping;
You have done your utmost part:
Leave it with a quiet heart:
It will grow while you are sleeping.

"But, O father," says the child,
With a troubled face up-creeping,
"How can I but think and grieve
When the fierce wind comes at eve
Tearing it — and I lie sleeping!

"I have loved my young tree so!
In each bud seen leaf and floweret,
Water'd it each day with prayers,
Guarded it with many cares,
Lest some canker should devour it.

"O good father," sobs the child,
"If I come in summer's shining,
And my pretty tree be dead,
How the sun will scorch my head,
How I shall sit lorn, repining!

"Rather let me evermore,
An incessant watch thus keeping,
Bear the cold, the storm, the frost,
That my treasure be not lost —
Ay, bear aught — but idle sleeping."

Sternly said the father then,
"Who art thou, child, vainly grieving?
Canst *thou* send the balmy dews,
Or the rich sap interfuse
Through the dead trunk, inly living?

"Canst thou bid the heavens restrain
Natural tempests for thy praying?
Canst thou bend one tender shoot,
Urge the growth of one frail root,
Keep one leaflet from decaying?

"If it live to bloom all fair,
Will it praise *thee* for its blossom?
If it die, will any plaints

Reach thee, as with kings and saints
    Drops it to the cold earth's bosom?

"Plant it — all thou canst! — with prayers:
    It is safe 'neath His sky's folding
Who the whole earth compasses,
Whether we watch more or less,
    His wide eye all things beholding.

"Should He need a goodly tree
    For the shelter of the nations,
He will make it grow: if not,
Never yet His love forgot
    Human love, and faith, and patience.

"Leave thy treasure in His hand —
    Cease all watching and all weeping:
Years hence, men its shade may crave,
And its mighty branches wave
    Beautiful above thy sleeping."

If his hope, tear-sown, that child
    Garner'd after joyful reaping,
Know I not: yet unawares
Gleams this truth through many cares,
    "*It will grow while thou art sleeping.*"

SITTING ON THE SHORE.

The tide has ebb'd away:
No more wild dashings 'gainst the adamant rocks,
Nor swayings amidst sea-weed false that mocks
The hues of gardens gay:
No laugh of little wavelets at their play:
No lucid pools reflecting heaven's clear brow —
Both storm and calm alike are ended now.

The rocks sit grey and lone:
The shifting sand is spread so smooth and dry,
That not a tide might ever have swept by
Stirring it with rude moan:
Only some weedy fragments idly thrown
To rot beneath the sky, tell what has been:
But Desolation's self has grown serene.

Afar the mountains rise,
And the broad estuary widens out,
All sunshine; wheeling round and round about

Seaward, a white bird flies.
A bird? Nay, seems it rather in these eyes
A spirit, o'er Eternity's dim sea
Calling — "Come thou where all we glad souls be."

O life, O silent shore,
Where we sit patient; O great sea beyond
To which we turn with solemn hope and fond,
But sorrowful no more:
A little while, and then we too shall soar
Like white-wing'd sea-birds into the Infinite Deep:
Till then, Thou, Father — wilt our spirits keep.

EUDOXIA.

FIRST PICTURE.

O SWEETEST my sister, my sister that sits in the
sun,
Her lap full of jewels, and roses in showers on her
hair;
Soft smiling and counting her riches up slow, one by
one,
Cool-brow'd, shaking dew from her garlands — those
garlands so fair,
Many gasp, climb, snatch, struggle, and die for — *her*
every-day wear!
O beauteous my sister, turn downwards those mild
eyes of thine,
Lest they stab with their smiling, and blister or scorch
where they shine.

Young sister who never yet sat for an hour in the
cold,

Whose cheek scarcely feels half the roses that throng
to caress,
Whose light hands hold loosely these jewels and silver
and gold,
Remember thou those in the world who for ever on
press
In perils and watchings, and hunger and nakedness,
While thou sit'st content in this sunlight that round
thee doth shine.
Take heed! these have long borne their burthen —
now lift thou up thine.

Be meek — as befits one whose cup to the brim is
love-crown'd,
While others in dry dust drop empty — What, what
canst thou know
Of the wild human tide that goes sweeping eternally
round
The isle where thou sit'st pure and calm as a statue
of snow,
Around which good thoughts like kind angels con-
tinually go?
Be pitiful. *Whose* eyes once turn'd from the angels
to shine
Upon publicans, sinners? O sister, 't will not pol-
lute thine.

Who, even-eyed, looks on His children, the black and the fair,
The loved and the unloved, the tempted, untempted — marks all,
And metes — not as man metes? If thou with weak tender hand dare
To take up His balances — say where His justice should fall,
Far better be Magdalen dead at the gate of thy hall —
Dead, sinning, and loving, and contrite, and par-don'd, to shine
Midst the saints high in heaven, than thou, angel sister of mine!

EUDOXIA.

SECOND PICTURE.

O DEAREST my sister, my sister who sits by the hearth,
With lids softly drooping, or lifted up saintly and calm,
With household hands folded, or open'd for help and for balm,
And lips, ripe and dewy, or ready for innocent mirth,—
Thy life rises upwards to heaven every day like a psalm
Which the singer sings sleeping, and waked, would half wondering say—
"I sang not. Nay, how could I sing thus?—I only do pray."

O gentlest my sister, who walks in at every dark door

Whether bolted or open, unheedful of welcome or
frown ;
But entering silent as sunlight, and there sitting
down,
Illumines the damp walls and shines pleasant shapes
on the floor,
And unlocks dim chambers where low lies sad Hope,
without crown,
Uplifts her from sackcloth and ashes and black
mourning weeds,
Re-crowns and re-clothes her. — Then, on to the
next door that needs.

O blessed my sister, whose spirit so wholly dost live
In loving, that even the word "loved," with its rap-
turous sound,
Rings faintly, like earth-tunes when angels are hym-
ning around :
Whose eyes say : "Less happy methinks to receive
than to give." —
So whatsoever we give, may One give to thee with-
out bound,
All best gifts — all dearest gifts — whether His right
hand do close
Or open — He holds it for ever above thee ; — He
knows !

EUDOXIA.

THIRD PICTURE.

O SILENT my sister, who stands by my side at the shore,
Back gazing with me on those waves which we mortals call years,
That rose, grew, and threaten'd, and climax'd, and broke, and were o'er,
While we still sit watching and watching, our cheeks free from tears —
O sister, with looks so familiar, yet strange, flitting by,
Say, say, hast thou been to those dead years as faithful as I?

Have they cast at thy feet also, jewels and whitening bones,
Gold, silver, and wreck-wood, dank sea-weed and treasures of cost?

Hast thou buried thy dead, sought thy jewels 'midst shingle and stones,
And learnt how the lost is the found, and the found is the lost?
Or stood with clear eyes upturn'd placid 'twixt sorrow and mirth,
As asking deep questions that cannot be answer'd on earth? —

I know not. Who knoweth? Our own souls we scarcely do know,
And none knows his brother's. Who judges, contemns, or bewails,
Or mocketh, or praiseth? In this world's strange vanishing show,
The one truth is *loving.* O sister, the dark cloud that veils
All life, lets this rift through to glorify future and past.
"Love ever — love only — love faithfully — love to the last."

BENEDETTA MINELLI.

I.

THE NOVICE.

It is near morning. Ere the next night fall
  I shall be made the bride of heaven. Then home
  To my still marriage chamber I shall come,
And spouseless, childless, watch the slow years crawl.

These lips will never meet a softer touch
  Than the stone crucifix I kiss; no child
  Will clasp this neck. Ah, virgin-mother mild,
Thy painted bliss will mock me overmuch.

This is the last time I shall twist the hair
  My mother's hand wreath'd, till in dust she lay:
  The name, her name, given on my baptism-day,
This is the last time I shall ever bear.

O weary world, O heavy life, farewell!
  Like a tired child that creeps into the dark

To sob itself asleep, where none will mark, —
So creep I to my silent convent cell.

Friends, lovers whom I loved not, kindly hearts
Who grieve that I should enter this still door,
Grieve not. Closing behind me evermore,
Me from all anguish, as all joy, it parts.

Love, whom alone I loved; who stand'st far off,
Lifting compassionate eyes that could not save,
Remember, this my spirit's quiet grave
Hides me from worldly pity, worldly scoff.

'T was less thy hand than Heaven's which came between,
And dash'd my cup down. See, I shed no tears:
And if I think at all of vanish'd years,
'T is but to bless thee, dear, for what has been.

My soul continually does cry to thee;
In the night watches ghost-like stealing out
From its flesh tomb, and hovering thee about;
So live that I in heaven thy face may see!

Live, noble heart, of whom this heart of mine
Was half unworthy. Build up actions great,

That I down looking from the crystal gate
Smile o'er our dead hopes urn'd in such a shrine.

Live, keeping aye thy spirit undefiled,
That when we stand before our Master's feet,
I with an angel's love may crown complete
The woman's faith, the worship of the child.

Dawn, solemn bridal morn; ope, bridal door,
I enter. My vow'd soul may Heaven now take;
My heart its virgin spousal for thy sake,
O love, keeps sacred thus for evermore.

BENEDETTA MINELLI.

II.

THE SISTER OF MERCY.

Is it then so? — Good friends, who sit and sigh
  While I lie smiling, are my life's sands run?
  Will my next matins, hymn'd beyond the sun,
Mingle with those of saints and martyrs high?

Shall I with these my grey hairs turn'd to gold,
  My aged limbs new clad in garments white,
  Stand all transfigured in the angels' sight,
Singing triumphantly that moan of old, —

Thy will be done. It was done. O my God,
  Thou know'st, when over grief's tempestuous sea
  My broken-wingèd soul fled home to Thee,
I writhed, but never murmur'd at Thy rod.

It fell upon me, stern at first, then soft
  As parent's kisses, till the wound was heal'd;
  And I went forth a labourer in Thy field:—
They best can bind who have been bruisèd oft.

And Thou wert pitiful. I came heart-sore,
  And drank Thy cup because earth's cups ran dry:
  Thou slew'st me not for that impiety,
But madest the draught so sweet, I thirst no more.

I came for silence, heavy rest, or death:
  Thou gavest instead life, peace, and holy toil:
  My sighing lips from sorrow didst assoil,
And fill with righteous thankfulness each breath.

Therefore I praise Thee that Thou shuttest Thine ears
  Unto my misery: didst Thy will, not mine:
  That to this length of days Thy hand divine,
My feet from falling kept, mine eyes from tears.

Sisters, draw near. Hear my last words serene:
  When I was young I walk'd in mine own ways,
  Worshipp'd—not God: sought not alone His praise;
So He cut down my gourd while it was green.

And then He o'er me threw His holy shade,
  That though no other mortal plants might grow,
  Mocking the beauty that was long laid low,
I dwelt in peace, and His commands obey'd.

I thank Him for all joy and for all pain:
  For healèd pangs, for years of calm content:
  For blessedness of spending and being spent
In His high service where all loss is gain.

I bless Him for my life and for my death;
  But most, that in my death my life is crown'd,
  Since I see there, with angels gathering round,
My angel. Ay, love, thou hast kept thy faith,

I mine. The golden portals will not close
  Like those of earth, between us. Reach thy hand!
  No *miserere,* sisters. Chant out grand
Te Deum laudamus. Now — 't is all repose.

A DREAM OF DEATH.

"WHERE shall we sail to-day?" — Thus said, methought,
A voice, that only could be heard in dreams:
And on we glided without mast or oar,
A wondrous boat upon a wondrous sea.

Sudden, the shore curved inward to a bay,
Broad, calm, with gorgeous sea-weeds waving slow
Beneath the water, like rich thoughts that stir
In the mysterious deep of poets' hearts.

So still, so fair, so rosy in the dawn
Lay that bright bay: yet something seem'd to breathe,
Or in the air, or from the whispering waves,
Or from that voice, as near as one's own soul,

"*There was a wreck last night.*" A wreck? then where
The ship, the crew? — The all-entombing sea
On which is writ nor name nor chronicle
Laid itself o'er them with smooth crystal smile.

"*Yet was the wreck last night.*" And gazing down
Deep down below the surface, we were ware
Of ghastly faces with their open eyes
Uplooking to the dawn they could not see.

One moved with moving sea-weeds: one lay prone,
The tinted fishes gliding o'er his breast;
One, caught by floating hair, rock'd quietly
Upon his reedy cradle, like a child.

"The wreck has been" — said the melodious voice,
"Yet all is peace. The dead, that, while we slept,
Struggled for life, now sleep and fear no storms:
O'er them let us not weep when heaven smiles."

So we sail'd on above the diamond sands,
Bright sea-flowers, and white faces stony calm,
Till the waves bore us to the open main,
And the great sun arose upon the world.

A DREAM OF RESURRECTION.

So heavenly beautiful it lay,
  It was less like a human corse
  Than that fair shape in which perforce
A lost hope clothes itself alway.

The dream show'd very plain: the bed
  Where that known unknown face reposed —
  A woman's face with eyelids closed,
A something precious that was dead;

A something, lost on this side life,
  By which the mourner came and stood,
  And laid down, ne'er to be indued,
All flaunting robes of earthly strife;

Shred off, like votive locks of hair,
  Youth's ornaments of pride and strength,
  And cast them in their golden length
The silence of that bier to share.

No tears fell — but with gazings long
  Lorn memory tried to print that face
  On the heart's ever-vacant place,
With a sun-finger, sharp and strong. —

Then kisses, dropping without sound,
  And solemn arms wound round the dead,
  And lifting from the natural bed
Into the coffin's strange new bound.

Yet still no farewell, or belief
  In death, no more than one believes
  In some dread truth that sudden weaves
The whole world in a shroud of grief.

And still unanswer'd kisses ; still
  Warm clingings to the image cold
  With an incredulous faith's close fold,
Creative in its fierce "*I will.*"

Hush — hush ! the marble eyelids move,
  The kiss'd lips quiver into breath :
  Avaunt, thou mockery of Death !
Avaunt ! — we are conquerors, I and Love.

Corpse of dead Hope, awake, arise,
  A living Hope that only slept

Until the tears thus overwept
Had wash'd the blindness from our eyes.

Come back into the upper day:
Pluck off these cerements. Patient shroud,
We 'll wrap thee as a garment proud
Round the fair shape we thought was clay.

Clasp, arms; cling, soul; eyes, drink anew
The beauty that returns with breath:
Faith, that out-loved this trance-like death,
May see this resurrection too.

ON THE CLIFF–TOP.

FACE upward to the sky
Quiet I lie:
Quiet as if the finger of God's will
Had bade this human mechanism "be still!"
And sent the intangible essence, this strange *I*,
All wondering forth to His eternity.

Below, the sea's sound, faint
As dying saint
Telling of gone-by sorrows long at rest:
Above, the fearless sea-gull's shimmering breast
Painted a moment on the dark blue skies —
A hovering joy, that while I watch it flies.

Alike unheeded now
Old griefs, and thou
Quick-wingèd Joy, that like a bird at play
Pleasest thyself to visit me to-day:
On the cliff-top, earth dim and heaven clear,
My soul lies calmly, above hope — or fear.

But not — (do Thou forbid
Whose stainless lid
Wept tears at Lazarus' grave, and looking down
Afar off, upon Solyma's doom'd town.)
Ah, not above *love* — human yet divine —
Which, Thee seen first, in Thee sees all of Thine!

Is 't sunset? The keen breeze
Blows from the seas:
And at my side a pleasant vision stands
With her brown eyes and kind extended hands.
Dear, we 'll go down together and full fain
From the cliff-top to the busy world again.

AN EVENING GUEST.

If in the silence of this lonely eve
With the street lamp pale flickering on the wall,
An angel were to whisper me — "Believe —
It shall be given thee. Call!" — whom should I call?

And then I were to see thee gliding in
Clad in known garments, that with empty fold
Lie in my keeping, and my fingers, thin
As thine were once, to feel in thy safe hold:

"I should fall weeping on thy neck and say,
"I have so suffer'd since — since" — But my tears
Would stop, remembering how thou count'st thy day,
A day that is with God a thousand years.

Then what are these sad days, months, years of mine,
To thine eternity of full delight?

What my whole life, when myriad lives divine
  May wait, each leading to a higher height?

I lose myself — I faint. Beloved, best,
  Let me still dream, thy dear humanity
Sits with me here, my head upon thy breast,
  And then I will go back to heaven with thee.

AFTER SUNSET.

Rest — *rest* — four little letters, one short word,
Enfolding an infinitude of bliss —
Rest is upon the earth. The heavy clouds
Hang poised in silent ether, motionless,
Seeking nor sun nor breeze. No restless star
Thrills the sky's grey-robed breast with pulsing rays.
The night's heart has throbb'd out.
No grass blade stirs,
No downy-wingèd moth comes flittering by
Caught by the light — Thank God, there is no light,
No open-eyed, loud-voiced, quick-motion'd light,
Nothing but gloom and rest.
A row of trees
Along the hill horizon, westward, stands
All black and still, as if it were a rank
Of fallen angels, melancholy met
Before the amber gate of Paradise —
The bright shut gate, whose everlasting smile
Deadens despair to calm.

O, better far
Better than bliss is rest! If suddenly
Those burnish'd doors of molten gold, steel-barr'd,
Which the sun closed behind him as he went
Into his bridal chamber — were to burst
Asunder with a clang, and in a breath
God's mysteries were reveal'd — His kingdom came —
The multitudes of heavenly messengers
Hastening throughout all space — the thunder quire
Of praise — the obedient lightnings' lambent gleam
Around the unseen Throne — should I not sink
Crush'd by the weight of such beatitudes,
Crying, "Rest, only rest, thou merciful God!
Hide me within the hollow of Thy hand
In some dark corner of the universe,
Thy bright, full, busy universe, that blinds,
Deafens, and tortures — Give me only *rest!*"

O for a soul-sleep, long and deep and still!
To lie down quiet after the weary day,
Dropping all pleasant flowers from the numb'd hands,
Bidding good-night to all companions dear,
Drawing the curtains on this darken'd world,
Closing the eyes, and with a patient sigh
Murmuring "Our Father" — fall on sleep, till dawn!

THE GARDEN-CHAIR.

Two Portraits.

A PLEASANT picture, full of meanings deep,
Old age, calm sitting in the July sun,
On wither'd hands half-leaning — feeble hands,
That after their life-labours, light or hard,
Their girlish broideries, their marriage-ring'd
Domestic duties, their sweet cradle cares,
Have dropp'd into the quiet-folded ease
Of fourscore years. How peacefully the eyes
Face us! Contented, unregretful eyes,
That carry in them the whole tale of life
With its one moral — "Thus all was — thus best."
Eyes now so near unto their closing mild
They seem to pierce direct through all that maze,
As eyes immortal do.

Here — Youth. She stands
Under the roses, with elastic foot
Poised to step forward; eager-eyed, yet grave

Beneath the mystery of the unknown To-come,
Though longing for its coming. Firm prepared
(So say the lifted head and close, sweet mouth)
For any future: though the dreamy hope
Throned on her girlish forehead, whispers fond,
"Surely they err who say that life is hard;
Surely it shall not be with me as these."

God knows: He only. And so best, dear child,
Thou woman-statured, sixteen-year-old child,
Meet bravely the impenetrable Dark
Under thy roses. Bud and blossom thou
Fearless as they — if thou art planted safe,
Whether for gathering or for withering, safe
In the King's garden.

AN OLD IDEA.

STREAM of my life, dull, placid river, flow!
I have no fear of the engulphing seas:
Neither I look before me nor behind,
But lying mute with wave-dipp'd hand, float on.

It was not always so. My brethren, see
This oar-stain'd, trembling palm. It keeps the sign
Of youth's mad wrestling with the waves that drift
Immutably, eternally along.

I would have had them flow through fields and
flowers,
Giving and taking freshness, perfume, joy;
It winds through—here. Be silent, O my soul!
—The finger of God's wisdom drew its line.

So I lean back and look up to the stars,
And count the ripples circling to the shore,
And watch the solemn river rolling on
Until it widen to the open seas.

PARABLES.

"Hold every mortal joy
With a loose hand."

We clutch our joys as children do their flowers;
We look at them, but scarce believe them ours,
Till our hot palms have smirch'd their colours rare
And crush'd their dewy beauty unaware.

But the wise Gardener, whose they were, comes by
At hours when we expect not, and with eye
Mournful yet sweet, compassionate though stern,
Takes them.
Then in a moment we discern
By loss, what was possession, and half wild
With misery, cry out like angry child:
"O cruel! thus to snatch my posy fine!"
He answers tenderly, "Not thine, but mine,"
And points to those stain'd fingers which do prove
Our fatal cherishing, our dangerous love;
At which we, chidden, a pale silence keep;
Yet evermore must weep, and weep, and weep.

So on through gloomy ways and thorny brakes,
Quiet and slow, our shrinking feet he takes,
Led by the soilèd hand, which, laved in tears,
More and more clean beneath his sight appears.
At length the heavy eyes with patience shine —
"I am content. Thou took'st but what was thine."

And then he us his beauteous garden shows,
Where bountiful the Rose of Sharon grows:
Where in the breezes opening spice-buds swell,
And the pomegranates yield a pleasant smell:
While to and fro peace-sandalled angels move
In the pure air that they — not we — call Love:
An air so rare and fine, our grosser breath
Cannot inhale till purified by death.
And thus we, struck with longing joy, adore,
And satisfied, wait mute without the door,
Until the gracious Gardener maketh sign,
"Enter in peace. All this is mine — and thine."

LETTICE.

I SAID to Lettice, our sister Lettice,
  While droop'd and glisten'd her eyelash brown,
"Your man 's a poor man, a cold and dour man,
  There 's many a better about our town." —
She smiled securely — "He loves me purely:
  A true heart 's safe, both in smile or frown;
And nothing harms me while his love warms me,
  Whether the world go up or down."

"He comes of strangers, and they are rangers,
  And ill to trust, girl, when out of sight:
Fremd folk may blame ye, and e'en defame ye —
  A gown oft handled looks seldom white."
She raised serenely her eyelids queenly, —
  "My innocence is my whitest gown;
No harsh tongue grieves me while he believes me,
  Whether the world go up or down."

"Your man 's a frail man, was ne'er a hale man,
  And sickness knocketh at every door,

And death comes making bold hearts cower, breaking — "
Our Lettice trembled ; — but once, no more.
" If death should enter, smite to the centre
Our poor home palace, all crumbling down,
He cannot fright us, nor disunite us,
Life bears Love's cross, death brings Love's crown."

A SPIRIT PRESENT.

If, coming from that unknown sphere
  Where I believe thou art —
The world unseen which girds our world
  So close, yet so apart, —
Thy soul's soft call unto my soul
  Electrical could reach,
And mortal and immortal blend
  In one familiar speech, —

What wouldst thou say to me? wouldst ask
  What, since did me befall?
Or close this chasm of cruel years
  Between us — knowing all?
Wouldst love me — thy pure eyes seeing that
  God only saw beside?
Oh, love me! 'T was so hard to live,
  So easy to have died.

If while this dizzy whirl of life
  A moment pausing stay'd,

I face to face with thee could stand,
  I would not be afraid:
Not though from heaven to heaven thy feet
  In glad ascent have trod,
While mine took through earth's miry ways
  Their solitary road.

We could not lose each other. World
  On world piled ever higher
Would part like bank'd clouds, lightning-cleft
  By our two souls' desire.
Life ne'er divided us; death tried,
  But could not; Love's voice fine
Call'd luring through the dark — then ceased,
  And I am wholly thine.

A WINTER WALK.

We never had believed, I wis,
  At primrose time when west winds stole
  Like thoughts of youth across the soul,
In such an alter'd time as this,

When if one little flower did peep
  Up through the brown and sullen grass,
  We should just look on it, and pass
As if we saw it in our sleep.

Feeling as sure as that this ray
  Which cottage children call the sun,
  Colours the pale clouds one by one, —
Our touch would make it drop to clay.

We never could have look'd, in prime
  Of April, or when July trees
  Shook full-leaved in the evening breeze,
Upon the face of this pale time,

Still, soft, familiar; shining bleak
  On naked branches, sodden ground,
  Yet shining — as if one had found
A smile upon a dead friend's cheek,

Or old friend, lost for years, had strange
  In alter'd mien come sudden back,
  Confronting us with our great lack —
Till loss seem'd far less sad than change.

Yet though, alas! Hope did not see
  This winter skeleton through full leaves,
  Out of all bareness Faith perceives
Possible life in field and tree.

In bough and trunk the sap will move,
  And the mould break o'er springing flowers;
  Nature revives with all her powers,
But only nature; — never love.

So, listlessly with linkèd hands
  Both Faith and Hope glide soft away;
  While in long shadows, cool and grey,
The sun sets o'er the barren lands.

"WILL SAIL TO-MORROW."

THE good ship lies in the crowded dock,
Fair as a statue, firm as a rock:
Her tall masts piercing the still blue air,
Her funnel glittering white and bare,
Whence the long soft line of vapoury smoke
Betwixt sky and sea like a vision broke,
Or slowly o'er the horizon curl'd
Like a lost hope fled to the other world:
  She sails to-morrow —
  Sails to-morrow.

Out steps the captain, busy and grave,
With his sailor's footfall, quick and brave,
His hundred thoughts and his thousand cares,
And his steady eye that all things dares:
Though a little smile o'er the kind face dawns
On the loving brute that leaps and fawns,
And a little shadow comes and goes,
As if heart or fancy fled — where, who knows?
  He sails to-morrow:
  Sails to-morrow.

To-morrow the serried line of ships
Will quick close after her as she slips
Into the unknown deep once more:
To-morrow, to-morrow, some on shore
With straining eyes shall desperate yearn —
"This is not parting? return — return!"
Peace, wild-wrung hands! hush, sobbing breath!
Love keepeth its own through life and death;
    Though she sails to-morrow —
    Sails to-morrow.

Sail, stately ship; down Southampton water
Gliding fair as old Nereus' daughter:
Christian ship that for burthen bears
Christians, speeded by Christian prayers;
All kind angels follow her track!
Pitiful God, bring the good ship back!
All the souls in her for ever keep
Thine, living or dying, awake or asleep:
    Then sail to-morrow!
    Ship, sail to-morrow!

AT EVEN-TIDE.

C. N. — Died, April 1857.

WHAT spirit is it that doth pervade
  The silence of this empty room?
And as I lift my eyes, what shade
  Glides off and vanishes in gloom?

I could believe this moment gone,
  A known form fill'd that vacant chair,
That those kind eyes upon me shone
  I never shall see anywhere!

The living are so far away:
  But *thou* — thou seemest strangely near;
Knowest all my silent heart would say,
  Its peace, its pain, its hope, its fear.

And from thy calm supernal height,
  And wondrous wisdom newly won,

Smilest on all our poor delight,
  And petty woe beneath the sun.

From all this coil thou hast slipp'd away,
  As softly as a cloud departs
Along the hill-side purple grey —
  Into the heaven of patient hearts.

Nothing here suffer'd, nothing miss'd,
  Will ever stir from its repose
The death-smile on her lips unkiss'd,
  Who all things loves and all things knows.

And I, who, ignorant and weak,
  Of love so helpless — quick to pain,
With restless longing ever seek
  The unattainable in vain.

Find it strange comfort thus to sit
  While the loud world unheeded rolls,
And clasp, ere yet the fancy flit,
  A friend's hand from the land of souls.

A DEAD SEA-GULL.

Near Liverpool.

LACK-LUSTRE eye, and idle wing,
And smirchèd breast that skims no more,
White as the foam itself, the wave —
Hast thou not even a grave
Upon the dreary shore,
Forlorn, forsaken thing?

Thou whom the deep seas could not drown,
Nor all the elements affright,
Flashing like thought across the main,
Mocking the hurricane,
Screaming with shrill delight
When the great ship went down.

Thee not thy beauty saved, nor mirth,
Nor daring, nor thy humble lot,
One among thousands — in quick haste

Fate clutch'd thee as she past;
Dead — how, it matters not:
Corrupting, earth to earth.

And not a league from where it lies
Lie bodies once as free from stain,
And hearts as gay as this sea-bird's,
Whom all the preachers' words
Will ne'er make white again,
Or from the dead to rise.

Rot, pretty bird, in harmless clay: —
We sing too much poetic woes;
Let us be doing while we can:
Blessed the Christian man
Who on life's shore seeks those
Dying of soul decay.

LOOKING EAST

In January, 1858.

Little white clouds, why are you flying
  Over the sky so blue and cold?
Fair faint hopes, why are you lying
  Over my heart like a white cloud's fold?

Slender green leaves, why are you peeping
  Out of the ground where the snow yet lies?
Toying west wind, why are you creeping
  Like a child's breath across my eyes?

Hope and terror by turns consuming,
  Lover and friend put far from me, —
What should *I* do with the bright spring, coming
  Like an angel over the sea?

Over the cruel sea that parted
  Me from mine own, and rolls between; —

Out of the woful east, whence darted
  Heaven's full quiver of vengeance keen.

Day teaches day, night whispers morning —
  "Hundreds are weeping their dead, while thou
Weeping thy living — Rise, be adorning
  Thy brows, unwidow'd, with smiles." — But how?

Oh, had he married me! — unto anguish
  Hardship, sickness, peril, and pain;
That on my breast his head might languish
  In lonely jungle or scorching plain;

Oh, had we stood on some rampart gory,
  Till he — ere Horror behind us trod —
Kiss'd me, and kill'd me — so, with his glory
  My soul went happy and pure to God!

Nay, nay, heaven pardon me! me, sick-hearted,
  Living this long, long life-in-death:
Many there are far wider parted
  Who under one roof-tree breathe one breath.

But we that *loved* — whom one word half-broken
  Had drawn together close soul to soul
As lip to lip — and it was not spoken,
  Nor may be while the world's ages roll.

I sit me down with my tears all frozen:
  I drink my cup, be it gall or wine:
For I know, if he lives, I am his chosen —
  I know, if he dies, that he is mine.

If love in its silence be greater, stronger
  Than million promises, sighs, or tears —
I will wait upon Him a little longer
  Who holdeth the balance of our years.

Little white clouds like angels flying,
  Bring the spring with you across the sea —
Loving or losing, living or dying,
  Lord, remember, remember me!

OVER THE HILLS AND FAR AWAY.

A LITTLE bird flew my window by,
'Twixt the level street and the level sky,
The level rows of houses tall,
The long low sun on the level wall;
And all that the little bird did say
Was "Over the hills and far away."

A little bird sang behind my chair,
From the level line of corn-fields fair,
The smooth green hedgerow's level bound
Not a furlong off — the horizon's bound,
And the level lawn where the sun all day
Burns: — "Over the hills and far away."

A little bird sings above my bed,
And I know if I could but lift my head
I would see the sun set, round and grand,
Upon level sea and level sand,
While beyond the misty distance grey
Is "Over the hills and far away."

I think that a little bird will sing
Over a grassy mound, next spring,
Where something that once was *me,* ye 'll leave
In the level sunshine, morn and eve:
But I shall be gone, past night, past day,
Over the hills and far away.

TOO LATE.

"Douglas, Douglas, tendir and treu."

COULD ye come back to me, Douglas, Douglas,
In the old likeness that I knew,
I would be so faithful, so loving, Douglas,
Douglas, Douglas, tender and true.

Never a scornful word should grieve ye,
I'd smile on ye sweet as the angels do; —
Sweet as your smile on me shone ever,
Douglas, Douglas, tender and true.

O to call back the days that are not!
My eyes were blinded, your words were few:
Do you know the truth now up in heaven,
Douglas, Douglas, tender and true?

I never was worthy of you, Douglas;
Not half worthy the like of you:
Now all men beside seem to me like shadows —
I love *you*, Douglas, tender and true.

Stretch out your hand to me, Douglas, Douglas,
  Drop forgiveness from heaven like dew;
As I lay my heart on your dead heart, Douglas,
  Douglas, Douglas, tender and true.

LOST IN THE MIST.

THE thin white snow-streaks pencilling
  That mountain's shoulder grey,
While in the west the pale green sky
  Smiled back the dawning day,
Till from the misty east the sun
  Was of a sudden born
Like a new soul in Paradise —
  How long it seems since morn!

One little hour, O round red sun,
  And thou and I shall come
Unto the golden gate of rest,
  The open door of home:
One little hour, O weary sun,
  Delay the threaten'd eve
Till my tired feet that pleasant door
  Enter and never leave.

Ye rooks that fly in slender file
  Into the thick'ning gloom,

Ye 'll scarce have reach'd your grim grey tower
  Ere I have reach'd my home;
Plover, that thrills the solitude
  With such an eerie cry,
Seek you your nest ere night-fall comes,
  As my heart's nest seek I.

O light, light heart and heavy feet,
  Patience a little while!
Keep the warm love-light in these eyes,
  And on these lips the smile:
Out-speed the mist, the gathering mist
  That follows o'er the moor! —
The darker grows the world without
  The brighter seems that door.

O door, so close yet so far off;
  O mist that nears and nears!
What, shall I faint in sight of home?
  Blinded — but not with tears —
'T is but the mist, the cruel mist,
  Which chills this heart of mine:
These eyes, too weak to see that light —
  It has not ceased to shine.

A little further, further yet:
  The white mist crawls and crawls;

It hems me round, it shuts me in
  Its great sepulchral walls:
No earth — no sky — no path — no light —
  A silence like the tomb:
Oh me, it is too soon to die —
  And I was going home!

A little further, further yet:
  My limbs are young, — my heart —
O heart, it is not only life
  That feels it hard to part:
Poor lips, slow freezing into calm,
  Numb'd hands that helpless fall,
And, a mile off, warm lips, fond hands,
  Waiting to welcome all!

I see the pictures in the room,
  The figures moving round,
The very flicker of the fire
  Upon the pattern'd ground:
O that I were the shepherd-dog
  That guards their happy door!
Or even the silly household cat
  That basks upon the floor!

O that I sat one minute's space
  Where I have sat so long!

O that I heard one little word
  Sweeter than angel's song!
A pause — and then the table fills,
  The harmless mirth brims o'er;
While I — oh *can* it be God's will? —
  I die, outside the door.

My body fails — my desperate soul
  Struggles before it go:
The bleak air 's full of voices wild,
  But not the voice I know;
Dim shapes come wandering through the dark:
  With mocking, curious stares
Faces long strange peer glimmering by —
  But not one face of theirs.

Lost, lost, and such a little way
  From that dear sheltering door
Lost, lost, out of the loving arms
  Left empty evermore!
His will be done. O, gate of heaven,
  Fairer than earthly door,
Receive me! Everlasting arms,
  Enfold me evermore!

And so, farewell * * * * * * * *
What is this touch

Upon my closing eyes?
My name too, that I thought to hear
Next time in Paradise?
Warm arms — close lips — Oh saved, saved, saved!
Across the deathly moor
Sought, found — and yonder through the night
Shineth the blessed door.

SEMPER FIDELIS.

"Mine own familiar friend, in whom I trusted."

THINK you, had we two lost fealty, something would
not, as I sit
With this book upon my lap here, come and over-
shadow it?
Hide with spectral mists the pages, under each familiar
leaf
Lurk, and clutch my hand that turns it with the icy
clutch of grief?

Think you, were we twain divided, not by distance,
time, or aught
That the world calls separation, but we smile at, better
taught,
That I should not feel the dropping of each link
you did untwine
Clear as if you sat before me with your true eyes
fixed on mine?

That I should not, did you crumble as the other
false friends do
To the dust of broken idols, know it without sight
of you,
By some shadow darkening daylight in the fickle skies
of spring,
By foul fears from household corners crawling over
everything?

If that awful gulf were opening which makes two,
however near,
Parted more than we were parted, dwelt we in each
hemisphere, —
Could I sit here, smiling quiet on this book within
my hand,
And while earth was cloven beneath me, feel no
shock nor understand?

No, you cannot, could not alter. No, my faith
builds safe on yours,
Rock-like; though the winds and waves howl, its
foundation still endures:
By a man's will — "See, I hold thee: mine thou
art, and mine shalt be."
By a woman's patience — "Sooner doubt I my own
soul than thee."

So, Heaven mend us! we'll together once again
take counsel sweet;
Though this hand of mine drops empty, that blank
wall my blank eyes meet:
Life may flow on: men be faithless, — ay forsooth
and women too!
One is true; and as He liveth, I believe in truth
— and *you.*

ONE SUMMER MORNING.

It is but a little while ago:
The elm-leaves have scarcely begun to drop away;
The sunbeams strike the elm-trunk just where they
struck that day —
Yet all seems to have happen'd long ago.

And the year rolleth round, slow, slow:
Autumn will fade to winter and winter melt in
spring,
New life return again to every living thing.
Soon, this will have happen'd long ago.

The bonnie wee flowers will blow;
The trees will re-clothe themselves, the birds sing
out amain, —
But never, never, never will the world look again
As it look'd before this happen'd — long ago!

MY LOVE ANNIE.

SOFT of voice and light of hand
As the fairest in the land —
Who can rightly understand
My love Annie?

Simple in her thoughts and ways,
True in every word she says, —
Who shall even dare to praise
My love Annie?

Midst a naughty world and rude
Never in ungentle mood;
Never tired of being good —
My love Annie.

Hundreds of the wise and great
Might o'erlook her meek estate;
But on her good angels wait,
My love Annie.

Many or few the loves that may
Shine upon her silent way, —
God will love her night and day,
My love Annie.

SUMMER GONE.

SMALL wren, mute pecking at the last red plum
    Or twittering idly at the yellowing boughs
    Fruit-emptied, over thy forsaken house, —
Birdie, that seems to come
Telling, we too have spent our little store,
Our summer 's o'er :

Poor robin, driven in by rain-storms wild
    To lie submissive under household hands
    With beating heart that no love understands,
And scarèd eye, like a child
Who only knows that he is all alone
And summer 's gone ;

Pale leaves, sent flying wide, a frighten'd flock
    On which the wolfish wind bursts out, and tears
    Those tender forms that lived in summer airs
Till, taken at this shock,
They, like weak hearts when sudden grief sweeps by,
Whirl, drop, and die : —

All these things, earthy, of the earth — do tell
 This earth's perpetual story; we belong
 Unto another country, and our song
Shall be no mortal knell;
Though all the year's tale, as *our* years run fast
Mourns, "summer 's past."

O love immortal, O perpetual youth,
 Whether in budding nooks it sits and sings
 As hundred poets in a hundred springs,
Or slaking passion's drouth
In wine-press of affliction, ever goes
Heavenward, through woes:

O youth immortal — O undying love!
 With these by winter fireside we 'll sit down
 Wearing our snows of honour like a crown;
And sing as in a grove,
Where the full nests ring out with happy cheer,
"Summer is here."

Roll round, strange years; swift seasons, come and go;
 Ye leave upon us but an outward sign;
 Ye cannot touch the inward and divine,
While God alone does know;
There seal'd till summers, winters, all shall cease
In His deep peace.

Therefore uprouse ye winds and howl your will;
 Beat, beat, ye sobbing rains on pane and door;
 Enter, slow-footed age, and thou, obscure
Grand Angel — not of ill;
Healer of every wound, where'er thou come
Glad, we 'll go home.

THE VOICE CALLING.

In the hush of April weather,
With the bees in budding heather,
And the white clouds floating, floating, and the sunshine falling broad:
While my children down the hill
Run and leap, and I sit still, —
Through the silence, through the silence art Thou calling, O my God?

Through my husband's voice that prayeth,
Though he knows not what he sayeth,
Is it Thou who in Thy holy Word hast solemn words for me?
And when he clasps me fast,
And smiles fondly o'er the past,
And talks, hopeful, of the future — Lord, do I hear only Thee?

Not in terror nor in thunder
Comes Thy voice, although it sunder

Flesh from spirit, soul from body, human bliss from human pain:
All the work that was to do,
All the joys so sweet and new
Which Thou shewed'st me in a vision — Moses-like — and hid'st again.

From this Pisgah, lying humbled,
The long desert where I stumbled
And the fair plains I shall never reach, seem equal, clear and far:
On this mountain-top of ease
Thou wilt bury me in peace;
While my tribes march onward, onward, unto Canaan and war.

In my boy's loud laughter ringing,
In the sigh more soft than singing
Of my baby girl that nestles up unto this mortal breast,
After every voice most dear
Comes a whisper — "Rest not here."
And the rest Thou art preparing, is it best, Lord, is it best?

"Lord, a little, little longer!"
Sobs the earth-love, growing stronger:

He will miss me, and go mourning through his solitary days.
And heaven were scarcely heaven
If these lambs which Thou hast given
Were to slip out of our keeping and be lost in the world's ways.

Lord, it is not fear of dying
Nor an impious denying
Of Thy will, which for evermore on earth, in heaven, be done:
But the love that desperate clings
Unto these my precious things
In the beauty of the daylight, and the glory of the sun.

Ah, Thou still art calling, calling,
With a soft voice unappalling;
And it vibrates in far circles through the everlasting years;
When Thou knockest, even so!
I will arise and go. —
What, my little ones, more violets? — Nay, be patient — mother hears.

THE WREN'S NEST.

I TOOK the wren's nest; —
Heaven forgive me!
Its merry architects so small
Had scarcely finish'd their wee hall,
That empty still and neat and fair
Hung idly in the summer air.
The mossy walls, the dainty door,
Where Love should enter and explore,
And Love sit carolling outside,
And Love within chirp multiplied; —
I took the wren's nest; —
Heaven forgive me!

How many hours of happy pains
Through early frosts and April rains,
How many songs at eve and morn
O'er springing grass and greening corn,
What labours hard through sun and shade
Before the pretty house was made!

One little minute, only one,
And she 'll fly back, and find it — gone!
I took the wren's nest:
Bird, forgive me!

Thou and thy mate, sans let, sans fear,
Ye have before you all the year,
And every wood holds nooks for you,
In which to sing and build and woo;
One piteous cry of birdish pain —
And ye 'll begin your life again,
And quite forget the lost, lost home
In many a busy home to come. —
But I? — Your wee house keep I must
Until it crumble into dust.
I took the wren's nest:
God forgive me!

A CHRISTMAS CAROL.

TUNE — "God rest ye, merry gentlemen."

God rest ye, merry gentlemen; let nothing you dismay,
For Jesus Christ, our Saviour, was born on Christmas-day.
The dawn rose red o'er Bethlehem, the stars shone through the grey,
When Jesus Christ, our Saviour, was born on Christmas-day.

God rest ye, little children; let nothing you affright,
For Jesus Christ, your Saviour, was born this happy night;
Along the hills of Galilee the white flocks sleeping lay,
When Christ, the Child of Nazareth, was born on Christmas-day.

God rest ye, all good Christians; upon this blessed morn
The Lord of all good Christians was of a woman born:
Now all your sorrows He doth heal, your sins He takes away;
For Jesus Christ, our Saviour, was born on Christmas-day.

THE MOTHER'S VISITS.

From the French.

LONG years ago she visited my chamber,
  Steps soft and slow, a taper in her hand;
Her fond kiss she laid upon my eyelids,
  Fair as an angel from the unknown land:
Mother, mother, is it thou I see?
Mother, mother, watching over me.

And yesternight I saw her cross my chamber,
  Soundless as light, a palm-branch in her hand;
Her mild eyes she bent upon my anguish,
  Calm as an angel from the blessed land;
Mother, mother, is it thou I see?
Mother, mother, art thou come for me?

A GERMAN STUDENT'S FUNERAL HYMN.

"Thou shalt call, and I will answer Thee: Thou wilt have a desire to the work of Thine hands."

WITH steady march across the daisy meadow,
  And by the churchyard wall we go;
But leave behind, beneath the linden shadow,
  One, who no more will rise and go:
Farewell, our brother, here sleeping in dust,
Till thou shalt wake again, wake with the just.

Along the street where neighbour nods to neighbour,
  Along the busy street we throng,
Once more to laugh, to live and love and labour,—
  But he will be remember'd long:
Sleep well, our brother, though sleeping in dust:
Shalt thou not rise again—rise with the just?

Farewell, true heart and kindly hand, left lying
  Where wave the linden branches calm;

'T is his to live, and ours to wait for dying,
  We win, while he has won, the palm;
Farewell, our brother! But one day, we trust,
Call — he will answer Thee, God of the just.

WESTWARD HO!

We should not sit us down and sigh,
  My girl, whose brow a fane appears,
Whose stedfast eyes look royally
  Backwards and forwards o'er the years—

The long long years of conquer'd time,
  The possible years unwon, that slope
Before us in the pale sublime
  Of lives that have more faith than hope.

We dare not sit us down and dream
  Fond dreams, as idle children do:
My forehead owns too many a seam,
  And tears have worn their channels through

Your poor thin cheeks, which now I take
  'Twixt my two hands, caressing. Dear,
A little sunshine for my sake!
  Although we 're far on in the year.

Though all our violets, sweet! are dead,
The primrose lost from fields we knew,
Who knows what harvests may be spread
For reapers brave like me and you?

Who knows what bright October suns
May light up distant valleys mild,
Where as our pathway downward runs
We see Joy meet us, like a child

Who, sudden, by the roadside stands,
To kiss the travellers' weary brows,
And lead them through the twilight lands
Safely unto their Father's house.

So, we 'll not dream, nor look back, dear!
But march right on, content and bold,
To where our life sets, heavenly clear,
Westward, behind the hills of gold.

THE END.

www.ingramcontent.com/pod-product-compliance
Lightning Source LLC
LaVergne TN
LVHW010235110826
845151LV00004B/1301

* 9 7 8 1 4 2 5 5 2 4 7 9 1 *